"This wise and biblically solid guide cuts beneat.
the gospel seizes the heart and transforms our desire to do more than merely
exist in community, and instead allows us to participate together in God's
merciful kindness."

> **Dan B. Allender**, Professor of Counseling Psychology and Founding
> President, The Seattle School of Theology and Psychology; author

"Using this resource is a no-brainer. It's a practical, biblical, gospel-saturated
study that connect the dots between community and the rich Christian life,
without losing anyone's attention! Pastors, your people will thank you for
using this small group study–and you will thank God for the fruit!"

> **Dave Harvey**, Pastor; author of *Am I Called?* and *When Sinners Say I Do*

"The word 'community' has become such a buzzword in Christian circles that
it has almost lost its meaning. Bob and Will bring us out of the land of the
buzzword and into the biblical definition and application of what it means
to share our lives in the church through the gospel. I highly recommend
this book."

> **Dr. Darrin Patrick**, Founder of The Journey, St. Louis, MO; author of
> *Church Planter: The Man, The Message, The Mission*

"Will Walker and Bob Thune offer probing questions to confront your small
group head-on with the transforming power of the gospel as it works through
a community. If you are looking for a resource that could bring real change
to the small group environment of your church, this is it."

> **Matt Carter**, Pastor of Preaching and Vision at the Austin Stone
> Community Church and coauthor of *The Real Win: A Man's Quest for
> Authentic Success*

"I'm a cynical old preacher who knows that real community in the church
is hard to come by. But Thune and Walker's gift to us of this wonderful and
practical small group resource gives this old preacher hope. It should be read
and underlined by every leader in the church. Use this small group resource
and then you, with me, will 'rise up and call them blessed.'"

> **Steve Brown**, Key Life radio program Bible teacher; author of *Three
> Free Sins*

"Everyone longs for community. And pastors long to shepherd churches that
are deeply, authentically communal. In *The Gospel-Centered Community*,
Robert Thune and Will Walker provide church planters, pastors, small group
leaders, and all Christians a clear, accessible tool for working through the
messy challenges of living in community, and for growing together as the
body of Christ."

> **Daniel Montgomery**, Lead Pastor, Sojourn Community Church,
> Louisville, KY

"This is an incredibly helpful resource for fostering gospel-centered community in your church. Whether you are planting a new church, or aiming to strengthen an existing community, you will find this resource profoundly valuable. The Christian life is not meant to be lived in isolation. This book will help you develop a healthy, biblical view of Christian community."

Ben Peays, Executive Director, The Gospel Coalition

"The *Gospel-Centered Community* is an incredible introduction and practical guide for helping us live out the radical implications of God's grace and love together. The gospel is personal, but it's definitely not private. Why do we need each other? How does grace reframe and refocus our relationships? What's the difference between an ingrown 'clubish' church, and a community of believers who are learning to live and love missionally? That's what this little gem is all about!"

Scotty Smith, Founding Pastor of Christ Community Church; Teacher in Residence at West End Community Church; author of *Everyday Prayers: 365 Days to a Gospel-Centered Faith*

"Thune and Walker's first small group study, *The Gospel-Centered Life*, had a profound and life-changing impact on our church. Our small groups worked through the book, and everyone responded with great enthusiasm. With the publication of *The Gospel-Centered Community*, it appears they've done it again. I'm certain this short volume will take us even deeper into what it means to live in a community fashioned by the gospel of grace. Every church that longs to experience the development of healthy, Christ-centered and gospel-shaped community should avail themselves of this excellent resource."

Sam Storms, Lead Pastor, Bridgeway Church, Oklahoma City, OK

"Thune and Walker deftly diagnose our tendencies to hide and isolate, and then show how gospel practices enable us to live in rich, real community. Loneliness is lethal and the faint hope we've harbored for more finds fulfillment in gospel-centered community.

Glenn Lucke, President, Docent Research Group; coauthor *Common Grounds: Conversations about the Things That Matter Most*

"We desperately need to apply the gospel to our life together so we can live out our calling to be 'the light of the world' and a 'city on the hill.' Thune and Walker give us an insightful, clear, easy-to-follow road map for applying the humility, kindness, and grace of our Lord Jesus Christ to our relationships at church and in our community."

Angelo Juliani, Church planter, Bridge Community Church (PCA), Philadelphia, PA

THE
GOSPEL-CENTERED
COMMUNITY

THE GOSPEL-CENTERED COMMUNITY

Robert H. Thune and Will Walker

Study Guide with Leader's Notes

New Growth Press

www.newgrowthpress.com

New Growth Press, Greensboro, NC 27404
www.newgrowthpress.com

Typesetting: Lisa Parnell, lparnell.com
Cover Design: Faceoutbooks, faceoutbooks.com

ISBN: 978-1-942572-89-3

Printed in the United States of America

26 25 24 23 22 21 20 19   6 7 8 9 10

CONTENTS

Section 1: The Foundation of Gospel-Centered Community

Section 2: The Fruit of Gospel-Centered Community

ACKNOWLEDGMENTS

We want to express our deep gratitude:

to the people of Coram Deo Church and Providence Church, who have labored with us in the work of the gospel, encouraged us in the truth of the gospel, and loved us with the love of the gospel;

to our friends at Serge—wise and seasoned mentors—whose rich "oral tradition" of gospel centrality permeates this work;

and to our fellow pastors in the Acts 29 Network, who are giving their lives to see this vision of gospel-centered community realized in the planting and renewal of churches across the globe.

To God alone be the glory.

INTRODUCTION

ABOUT SERGE

Serge never set out to write and publish curriculum. We are an international mission-sending organization that has always believed that the power and motive for mission is the gospel of grace at work in the life of a believer. However, along the way, we've also discovered that it's a lot harder to do cross-cultural, team-oriented ministry than we thought. Eventually, we started writing material to keep the gospel front and center in our own lives and relationships. Before long we had pastors and ministry leaders requesting gospel-centered materials for use in their churches and ministries.

Over the years, it's been our privilege to partner with friends who share our passion for the way the gospel transforms both believers and unbelievers alike. This study is the result of one such partnership. Like *The Gospel-Centered Life*, the study that precedes it, Bob Thune and Will Walker wrote *The Gospel-Centered Community* to help their churches grow in the gospel. We're partnering with them to publish it because we think it may do the same for you.

As a cross-denominational, reformed, sending agency with over 200 missionaries in 15 countries, Serge is always looking for people who are ready to take the next step in a missional lifestyle. If you'd like to learn more about our teaching, healing, and equipping ministries around the world and what might be right for you, please visit us at http://www. serge.org/mission. If you'd like to learn more about our gospel mentoring programs and the discipleship training that we offer here in the United States, you can find those details at http://www.serge.org/mentoring.

FROM THE AUTHORS

For over a decade now, we have been involved in forming and leading missional communities. We started out in campus ministry, helping young fraternity men become disciples of Jesus. Then we applied our experience to the realm of church planting, striving to build gospel-centered churches that would form people in the gospel and send them out on mission for the glory of God.

One thing we've learned in our years of ministry is that the gospel has to be at the center of Christian community. Without the gospel, community groups will always become unhealthy. Some will become ingrown and self-absorbed. Others will become busy and activist. Either way, they will lose their compelling power to display the glory and grace of God. Only with the gospel at the center can a community become a thriving nexus of gospel discipleship, rich fellowship, and Spirit-empowered mission.

It's one thing to see the need for gospel-centered community. It's another thing to know how to cultivate it. How do you take a church, a small group, or even a family and build a vibrant gospel culture within it? That's where we hope this study will help.

This study—The Gospel-Centered Community—is a follow-up to another work we produced a few years ago called The Gospel-Centered Life. That study focused on personal renewal dynamics. The current one seeks to apply those same renewal dynamics to a larger community. Through a combination of Bible study, reflection, discussion, and application, we want to help your community experience the transforming power of the gospel.

ABOUT THIS STUDY

The phrase "gospel-centered" has experienced a surge of popularity in recent years. Though we're thankful for this renewed interest in the gospel, we've encountered two problems with the popularity of this term:

1. Many people use the phrase as a junk drawer. Because all faithful Christians love the gospel, "gospel-centered" becomes a phrase that easily gets people nodding their heads—even if they don't fully comprehend it.

2. Many people use this term "aspirationally." They *aspire* to be gospel-centered, but they don't really know how to *get* there.

The Gospel-Centered Community has been written to help remedy both of these problems. By God's grace, we trust that this study will (1) deepen your comprehension of the gospel and (2) help you move from *aspiring toward* gospel-centered community to actually *being* a gospel-centered community.

This may be obvious, but *The Gospel-Centered Community* is meant to be studied in community. This is not a personal Bible study to work through on your own. It is communal content that's meant to be learned, processed, and critiqued within a group. It's appropriate for missional church-planting contexts, established churches, and parachurch or campus ministries. If your group already has a fairly gospel-centered culture, this study will deepen it. And if your group desperately needs gospel reform and renewal, this study will provide a great starting point. It's foundational material that will work in almost any context.

HOW THIS STUDY IS ORGANIZED

The Gospel-Centered Community contains nine lessons that are grouped into two major sections.

Section 1: The Foundation of Gospel-Centered Community

LESSON 1: CREATED FOR COMMUNITY

This lesson explores the theme of community through the redemptive storyline of Creation-Fall-Redemption-Consummation. How does being created in God's image provide the foundation for meaningful community? How does the fall destroy community? How does redemption in Jesus renew our capacity for community? And how does community provide the context for our ongoing transformation? This lesson lays the foundation for a biblical understanding of the gospel and community.

LESSON 2: HOW COMMUNITY SHAPES US IN THE GOSPEL

This lesson focuses on the way community exposes our sin and unbelief, pushing us into a deeper dependence on what Jesus accomplished for us in his death and resurrection. When we begin to see community as a means of spiritual formation, we see every struggle or problem we have in relationships as a "gospel opportunity"—a chance to believe the promises of the gospel more deeply and to rely on the Holy Spirit to change our hearts and lives in the ways God desires.

LESSON 3: HOW THE GOSPEL SHAPES COMMUNITY

In this lesson, we want to explore how the gospel empowers and enables deeper community. By "deeper" community we mean community in which relationships are increasingly shaped by the good things that come from trusting Jesus and the promises of the gospel: things like a growing trust, openness, humility, service, teachability, and accountability that reflect God's character and his intentions for human relationships. We're still working out the same concepts, just coming at them from a different angle. As a result of this lesson, your group should begin to confront some of the barriers to deeper, more life-giving community.

LESSON 4: FAITH WORKING THROUGH LOVE

This lesson is a "hinge point" in the study. It introduces the concept of "faith working through love" (Galatians 5:6). We will never love one another as God intends unless we understand how faith in the work of Christ provides the foundation and the motivation for love. This lesson establishes a core principle that we'll return to in Lessons 5 through 9.

Section 2: The Fruit of Gospel-Centered Community

LESSON 5: A JOYFUL COMMUNITY

In this lesson, we begin to look at some of the characteristic marks of gospel-centered community. The first—and perhaps the most important—is joy. If joy is missing from Christian community, it's a clear indication that something is amiss in our understanding of the gospel. This lesson will help us understand why the relationship between justification and sanctification is crucial to experiencing joy in Christ.

LESSON 6: A HUMBLE COMMUNITY

Another mark of a gospel-centered community is humility. To grow in humility, we need to identify the ways pride manifests itself in our lives, and we need to put pride to death by looking to Jesus as our example and experiencing his grace personally. This lesson seeks to help us understand biblical humility, become more humble people, and shape a more humble community that is eager to serve.

LESSON 7: AN HONEST COMMUNITY

Authentic community means being known "as we really are." But most of us are worried that others would not accept us or like us if they really knew us. So instead of letting our true selves be known, we hide behind a false self. The apostle John urges us to turn from this darkness, this denial of truth, and "walk in the light" instead. This lesson explores how the good news of the gospel frees us from slavery to the approval or disapproval of others. When we are confident in our identity in Christ, we are free to be known as we really are and to love others as they really are.

LESSON 8: A GRACE-FILLED COMMUNITY

A gospel-centered community is a grace-filled community. But sin has distorted our understanding and tainted our desires in this area. Sometimes we settle for a flimsy sort of "acceptance" that doesn't confront unbiblical beliefs or behaviors. In other situations we can make people earn our acceptance through their performance. Our deep dysfunction in this area is only healed when we allow the gospel to transform our hearts and lives. When we understand and believe that God accepts and forgives us in Christ, we gain a right understanding of what it means to accept and forgive each other.

LESSON 9: A MISSIONAL COMMUNITY

In this last lesson, we consider one final characteristic of a gospel-centered community: mission. A gospel-centered community is a community that is moving toward others as God has moved toward them. All Christians are called to leave their comfortable routines and move toward their neighbors who don't know Christ. The Father sent the Son; the Son sent the Spirit; and the Spirit sends the church. As those changed by the Spirit through the gospel, we are a "going" people, always moving toward others as God has moved toward us.

HOW TO USE THIS STUDY

Each lesson follows a similar format including these elements:

BIBLE CONVERSATION

We want to start by talking about the Bible together. As the name suggests, this section is designed to stimulate your thinking and prepare you and your group for the ideas that will be presented in each lesson.

ARTICLE

The written articles are the primary source of the teaching content for each lesson. They are short, clear teachings of the concepts being presented in the lesson. Each week, your group will take a few minutes and read the article out loud together.

DISCUSSION

This section is where we communally process the concepts being taught in the article. Often the discussion will work in conjunction with the next section (exercise) to help flesh out the teaching and apply it to our lives in concrete ways.

EXERCISE

Each exercise in this study is designed to help you make practical applications of the concepts being taught or help you understand the content at a deeper heart level. Be sure to allow enough time for your group to adequately work through and discuss the exercises as directed.

WRAP-UP

The wrap-up gives the leader the chance to answer any last-minute questions, reinforce ideas and, most importantly, spend a few minutes praying as a group.

WHAT TO EXPECT

EXPECT TO BE CHALLENGED . . .

Most of us have reduced the gospel to something much less than it is. As you work through each lesson, expect your thinking about the gospel to be challenged and expanded.

EXPECT THE HOLY SPIRIT . . .

to be the one ultimately responsible for the growth of your group, and for the change in each person's life—including your own. Relax and trust him.

EXPECT YOUR GROUP'S AGENDA TO INCLUDE . . .

an open, give-and-take discussion of the article, the questions, and the exercises. Also expect times of prayer at each meeting.

EXPECT STRUGGLE . . .

and don't be surprised to find that your group is a mixture of enthusiasm, hope, and honesty along with indifference, anxiety, skepticism, guilt, and covering up. We are all people who really need Jesus every day. So expect your group to be made up of people who wrestle with sin and have problems—people just like yourself!

EXPECT A GROUP LEADER . . .

who desires to serve you but who also needs Jesus as much as you do. No leader should be put on a pedestal, so expect that your group leader will have the freedom to share openly about his or her own weaknesses, struggles, and sins.

GOSPEL OVERVIEW

The study you are about to begin aims to help you live a "gospel-centered" life in a gospel-centered community. The obvious question is, What exactly is "the gospel"? That's a question we should clear up before going any further. Though many people are familiar with the word *gospel*, we're often fuzzy about its content.

Many popular "gospel presentations" distill the gospel message down to three or four core principles. These simple summaries can be very helpful. But a richer way to understand the gospel is as a *story*—the true Story that speaks to our purest aspirations and deepest longings. This Great Story has four chapters.

CREATION: THE WORLD WE WERE MADE FOR

The Story begins, not with us, but with God. Deep down, we have a sense that this is true. We sense that we are important—that there is something dignified, majestic, and eternal about humanity. But we also know that we are not ultimate. Something (or Someone) greater than us exists.

The Bible tells us that this Someone is the one infinite, eternal, and unchanging God who created all things out of nothing (Genesis 1:1–31). This one God exists in three persons—Father, Son, and Holy Spirit (Matthew 28:19). Because God is Triune in his being, he wasn't motivated to create the world because he *needed* something—be it relationship, worship, or glory. Rather, he created out of the overflow of his perfection—his own love, goodness, and glory. God made human beings in his image (Genesis 1:27), which is what gives us our dignity and value. He also made us *human*, which means we are created beings, dependent on our Creator. We were made to worship, enjoy, love, and serve him, not ourselves.

In God's original creation, everything was good. The world existed in perfect peace, stability, harmony, and wholeness.

FALL: THE CORRUPTION OF EVERYTHING

God created us to worship, enjoy, love, and serve him. But rather than live under God's authority, humanity turned away from God in sinful rebellion (Genesis 3:1–7; Isaiah 53:6). Our defection plunged the whole world into the darkness and chaos of sin. Though vestiges of good remain, the wholeness and harmony of God's original creation is shattered.

As a result, all human beings are sinners by nature and by choice (Ephesians 2:1–3). We often excuse our sin by claiming that we're "not that bad"—after all, we can always find someone worse than we are! But this evasion only reveals our shallow and superficial view of sin. Sin is not primarily an *action*; it's a *disposition*. It's our soul's aversion to God. Sin is manifested in our pride, our selfishness, our independence, and our lack of love for God and others. Sometimes sin is very obvious and external; other times it's hidden and internal. But "all have sinned and fall short of the glory of God" (Romans 3:23).

Sin brings two drastic consequences into our lives. First, *sin enslaves us* (Romans 6:17–18). When we turn *from* God, we turn *to* other things to find our life, our identity, our meaning, and our happiness. These things become substitute gods—what the Bible calls idols—and they soon enslave us, demanding our time, our energy, our loyalty, our money—everything we are and have. They begin to rule over our lives and hearts. This is why the Bible describes sin as something that "masters" us (Romans 6:14 NIV). Sin causes us to "serve created things rather than the Creator" (Romans 1:25 NIV).

Second, *sin brings condemnation*. We're not just enslaved by our sin; we're *guilty* because of it. We stand condemned before the Judge of heaven and earth. "The wages of sin is death" (Romans 6:23). We are under a death sentence for our cosmic treason against the holiness and justice of God. His righteous anger toward sin stands over us (Nahum 1:2; John 3:36).

REDEMPTION: JESUS COMES TO SAVE US

Every good story has a hero. And the hero of the Gospel Story is Jesus. Humanity needs a Savior, a Redeemer, a Deliverer to free us from the bondage and condemnation of sin and to restore the world to its original good. This Rescuer must be *truly human* in order to pay the debt we owe to God. But he can't be *merely human* because he must conquer sin. We need a Substitute—one who can live the life of obedience we've failed to live, and who can stand in our place to bear the punishment we deserve for our disobedience and sin.

This is why God sent Jesus into the world to be our substitute (1 John 4:14). The Bible teaches that Jesus was fully God—the second person of the Trinity—and also fully human. He was born to a human mother, lived a real flesh-and-blood existence, and died a brutal death on a Roman cross outside Jerusalem. Jesus lived a life of perfect obedience to God (Hebrews 4:15), making him the only person in history who did not deserve judgment. But on the cross, he took our place, dying for our sin. He received the condemnation and death we deserve so that, when we put our trust in him, we can receive the blessing and life he deserves (2 Corinthians 5:21).

Not only did Jesus die in our place, he rose from death, displaying his victory over sin, death, and hell. His resurrection is a decisive event in history; the Bible calls it the "first fruits"—the initial evidence—of the cosmic renewal God is bringing (1 Corinthians 15:20–28). One of the greatest promises in the Bible is Revelation 21:5: "Behold, I am making all things new." All that was lost, broken, and corrupted in the fall will ultimately be put right. Redemption doesn't simply mean the salvation of individual souls; it means the restoring of the whole creation back to its original good.

A NEW PEOPLE: THE STORY CONTINUES

So how do we become a part of the story? How do we experience God's salvation personally and become agents of his redemption in the world? By faith or trust (Ephesians 2:8–9). What does that mean? We trust a taxi driver when we count on him to get us to our destination. We trust a doctor when we agree with her diagnosis and entrust ourselves to her care. And we trust in Jesus Christ when we admit our sin, receive his gracious forgiveness, and rest entirely in Jesus for our acceptance before God. Faith is like getting in the taxi. It's like going under the surgeon's knife. It's a restful, whole-hearted commitment of the self to Jesus (Psalm 31:14–15). This is what it means to believe the gospel.

When we trust in Jesus, we are released from sin's condemnation *and* from its bondage. We are free to say "no" to sin and "yes" to God. We are free to die to ourselves and live for Christ and his purposes. We are free to work for justice in the world. We are free to stop living for our own glory and start living for the glory of God (1 Corinthians 10:31). We are free to love God and others in the way we live, which is the particular focus of this study.

God has promised that Jesus will return to finally judge sin and make all things new. Until then, he is gathering to himself a people "from every nation, tribe, people and language" (Revelation 7:9 NIV). As part of that called-and-sent people, we have the privilege of joining him in his mission (Matthew 28:18–20) as individuals and as part of his spiritual family. By grace, we can enjoy God, live life for his glory, serve humanity, and make his gospel known to others through our words and actions.

This is the good news—the True Story—of the gospel.

SECTION 1:
THE FOUNDATION OF GOSPEL-CENTERED COMMUNITY

1

CREATED FOR COMMUNITY

BIG IDEA

Community is something we all want. Every human being longs for meaningful relationships—a context in which they can know and be known. Theologically, this longing for community is rooted in God himself: God is a relational being (three persons in one as the Trinity), and we are made in his image. This lesson explores the theme of community through the grid of Creation-Fall-Redemption-Consummation. How does being created in God's image provide the foundation for meaningful community? How does the fall destroy community? How does redemption in Jesus renew our capacity for community? And how does community provide the context for our ongoing transformation? This lesson lays the foundation for a biblical understanding of the gospel and community.

NOTES:

CREATED FOR COMMUNITY

Community is something we all want.

No matter how you're wired—introvert, extrovert, socially adept or so-cially awkward—something in your soul longs for meaningful relation-ships with other humans. We long to know others and be known by them. We treasure friendships that allow us to truly "be ourselves." Though some of us have never found this sort of community and though others have been deeply wounded by relationships, all of us still long for deep, authentic, real community.

How did we get this way? How did this craving, this longing, get hard-wired into us? The Bible answers that question by explaining that we are created in the image of God. **God created us for community**.

CREATED FOR COMMUNITY

One of the oldest and most cherished doctrines of historic Christian theology is the doctrine of the Trinity. The Nicene Creed (c. AD 325) summarizes the Trinity this way:

> I believe in one God, the Father Almighty, Maker of heaven and earth, and of all things visible and invisible. And in one Lord Jesus Christ, the only-begotten Son of God, begotten of the Fa-ther before all worlds; God of God, Light of Light, very God of very God; begotten, not made, being of one substance with the

Father. . . . And I believe in the Holy Ghost, the Lord and Giver
of Life; who proceeds from the Father and the Son; who with
the Father and the Son together is worshipped and glorified.

The Trinity means that God himself is in community. More accurately,
God *is* community: one God, three persons. "Before all worlds"—before
any sort of human community existed—there was God, dwelling in perfect, loving harmony in his threefold being.

In the biblical account of creation, this Triune God says: "Let us make
man in our image" (Genesis 1:26). Human beings are made to *image* God,
to reflect his likeness. That's why our longing for community seems so
deep and primal. It's how we're made as God's image bearers.

So if deep community is something we all want, if it's part of being made
in God's image, then what makes it so hard to attain? What keeps us
from achieving the type of meaningful human relationships that God
wired us for?

THE FALL: BROKEN COMMUNITY

If you think for a moment about the nature of your relationships, you'll
quickly identify another tendency that's present—something darker and
more sinister than your God-given desire for community. It's the tendency
to use people to meet your own needs first. It's not hard to see how often we
are self-focused, pursuing our own interests and protecting ourselves from
people and relationships that will demand too much of us. For example,
think of the times you've intentionally avoided someone who bothers you.
Or the times you've said what people wanted to hear in order to avoid
offending them. Or the times you've stopped pursuing certain friends because they were no longer useful to you. Or the times you've clung to bad
or unhealthy relationships just to escape the feeling of being alone.

These selfish tendencies reveal that something has gone deeply wrong in
our pursuit of community. Though made in God's image, we have fallen
from our original glory. We have devolved into something less than what
we were made to be. There's something selfish and self-absorbed about
us that prevents us from imaging God the way we were designed to.

Our inherent selfishness is evidence of what the Bible calls "sin." When we hear the word *sin,* we tend to think of bad behavior. But sin is deeper than external actions. The Bible often talks about sin in terms of **unbelief**. In other words, rather than believing what is true, we believe lies, which obviously leads to bad behavior and negative emotions. Unbelief was at the root of the first sin. Eve believed the Serpent's lie about God and his intentions toward them: "You will not surely die. For God knows that when you eat of it [the forbidden fruit] your eyes will be opened, and you will be like God" (Genesis 3:4–5). Unbelief is a failure to see and believe what's true about God, the world, and ourselves. It's not taking God at his word, not believing his promises, not trusting in his goodness.

And sin's impact is not just that we *don't* believe, it's that apart from Christ we're *unable* to believe. Sin has turned us in on ourselves and warped our relationships with others. We need Someone who can deliver us from our unbelief and selfishness and restore our capacity for true, deep, lasting community.

REDEEMED FOR COMMUNITY

This is where the good news of the **gospel** meets us. The word *gospel* literally means "good news"—a message, a proclamation, an announcement. One of the paradoxes of this message is that before it can be good news, it must start with bad news: we are sinful, broken people. We are rebels against God. We are mired in lies and self-worship, and we look to things other than God to give us identity and significance. We can't free ourselves, make God happy with us, or do enough good works to make up for our sins. But God, rich in mercy, sent Jesus to earth as our substitute. Jesus took our place in his life as he obeyed God fully and worshiped him totally, things we failed to do. He substituted himself for us in his death, as he paid the penalty we owed to God for our sin and unbelief. If we humble ourselves, acknowledge our need, and turn to him, God the Holy Spirit will apply Jesus' substitutionary work to us by faith. The Bible calls this *redemption,* a word that means "to be delivered, ransomed, or set free."

What does Jesus redeem us *from*? Sin and all its effects. What does Jesus redeem us *for*? A life that images God and reflects his goodness to the world. In other words, one of the chief things that Jesus accomplishes when he redeems us is to restore our capacity for community. Not for a community of people who look and act just like us, but a community made up of people from every tribe and tongue and nation on earth (Revelation 7:9). God has created us for community, and Jesus has redeemed us for community. In doing so, he has made us into his very own body (1 Corinthians 12:27) that is able to live, love, and make known his "good news" to our friends and neighbors.

But wait: If Jesus redeems us for community, then why is community still such hard work? Why are relationships still fraught with brokenness, even among Christians? This is the tension we live in. Even though Jesus has delivered us from the penalty and rule of sin, he has not yet eradicated sin from the world. Because of sin's ongoing presence, we are prone to **unbelief**. We easily forget the good news of the gospel and fall back into lies and self-worship. That's why the Bible encourages us not just to receive the gospel, but to "stand" in it (1 Corinthians 15:1) and to "continue" in it (Colossians 1:23).

In other words, building and enjoying healthy community is going to require us to believe the gospel, to believe that what Jesus did for us has power and relevance for the way we relate to God and others. This requires an intentional focus on our part. It means identifying the unbelief in our hearts that hinders our ability to love and serve others and to receive love from them in turn. It means receiving the healing, liberating truths of the gospel in ways that allow them to soak deep into the core of our being. And guess where this work of ongoing transformation takes place? In community.

TRANSFORMED IN COMMUNITY

Did you ever notice how patient you are—as long as no one is getting on your nerves? Or how loving you are—as long as you're surrounded by people who are easy to love? Or how humble you are—as long as you're respected and admired by others? Every one of us is a saint in isolation! It's in community that our real weaknesses, flaws, and sins are exposed. That's why community is essential—not optional—for transformation. We can't become the people God wants us to become outside of community.

You see, redemption is not the end of the story. God is preparing us for "new heavens and a new earth, in which righteousness dwells" (2 Peter 3:13). His goal is a renewed creation, where redeemed humans dwell in perfect harmony with each other and with their Creator. God is out to prepare his people for this glorious future by transforming them now, a process the Bible calls *sanctification*. The agent of sanctification is the Holy Spirit. The tool of sanctification is the truth of the gospel. And the context of sanctification is community.

Consider some of the "one another" statements in the Bible: "Love one another with brotherly affection; outdo one another in showing honor" (Romans 12:10). "Comfort one another, agree with one another, live in peace" (2 Corinthians 13:11). "Do not use your freedom as an opportunity for the flesh, but through love serve one another" (Galatians 5:13). "Be kind to one another, tenderhearted, forgiving one another" (Ephesians 4:32). Isn't it obvious that none of us can do these things perfectly? These commands aren't given just so that we'll know what we *should* do; they're also given so that we can try, and fail, and grow in our experience of God's grace. Trying to fulfill these "one another" commands helps to reveal our sin, drives us to Jesus in repentance and faith, and causes us to depend on the Holy Spirit for transformation. Community is the laboratory in which we learn to rely on God's grace and experience the gospel's transforming power.

Community is also the primary context for *mission*, our outward focus as believers. God wants to use our communities, messy and broken as they are, to draw others into his story and introduce them to Jesus, the Redeemer! It's not just about us becoming more like Jesus; it's about people who don't know Jesus coming to know him as Savior and Lord.

We sometimes treat community like the safety net under a tightrope walker: it's a good thing to have in case something bad happens. But the Bible talks about community as if it's the tightrope itself: you can't move forward without it. We are created for community. We are redeemed for community. And we are transformed in community.

Lesson

1

EXERCISE

FIVE INDICATORS OF INDIVIDUALISM

In Western culture, individualism is like a windshield or a pair of glasses. We're so used to "seeing through" it that we don't even see it. We need some help to recognize how our self-centeredness actually manifests itself. Below are some indicators of individualism, some ways it may express itself based on who you are and how you're wired. Choose the one or two bullet-point statements below that you see most often in your life. (You may find bullet points that apply to you under multiple headings.)

SELF-RELIANCE

- You are proud of your ability to deal with your own problems and challenges without help from others.
- You enjoy being asked for help but you rarely ask others for help.
- It's difficult for you to be vulnerable about what's really going on in your soul because "those are my issues to deal with."
- You don't honestly think you need people to grow spiritually; personal spiritual disciplines are sufficient (Bible study, prayer, theological reading).
- It's hard for you to receive gifts or help from people without wanting to pay them back somehow.

SELF-SUFFICIENCY

- You may be thought of as a "good Christian" by others, but few people know you as you really are.
- You may be outgoing and extroverted, but your relationships stay on the surface.
- Very few people have full access to your life. You may disclose things to people, but only what you want them to know. You do not want them to dig deeper.
- When relationships get hard, you tend to withdraw rather than deal with the issues.
- You tend to measure spiritual growth by how much you know.

SELF-PROTECTION

- You tend to keep others at arm's length to guard against being hurt or rejected.
- You measure spiritual growth or maturity by what others say or think.
- You fear at times that if people knew "the real you," they would keep their distance.
- You avoid conflict. If people offend you or hurt your feelings, you prefer to say nothing rather than risk anger or rejection.
- You might be addicted to approval. Your sense of value rises and falls on what other people say (or do not say) about you.

SELF-IMPORTANCE

- You tend to be addicted to busyness; it's the way you fill the void of deep relationships in your life.
- You have a higher concern for respect from others (attention) than you have a sense of responsibility for others (sacrifice).
- You are more concerned about what others think of your accomplishments (importance) than what they think of your relational influence in their lives (significance).
- You tend to measure spiritual growth by what you have accomplished.

SELF-WILL

- You regularly choose work and hobbies over people.
- Your schedule and priorities always take precedence; you don't reshuffle your agenda to help or serve others.
- You like having people around, but you don't tend to take their advice or welcome their correction.
- When it comes to church, you tend to ask consumer-oriented questions like, "What do I like/not like? How does this make me feel? What do I get out of this?" Your wants and goals are functionally prioritized over the needs of the community and the mission of the church.

Notice that the headings over all of these bullet points have to do with "self." If your self-centeredness was transformed into a joyful God-centeredness, what would the results be for yourself and for the community around you?

HOW COMMUNITY SHAPES US IN THE GOSPEL

BIG IDEA

In the last lesson, we saw that we are created for community, redeemed for community, and transformed in community. We also observed that sin hinders community by making us self-centered and self-seeking. In this lesson, we want to see how community exposes our sin and unbelief, pushing us into a deeper dependence on what Jesus accomplished for us in his death and resurrection—the good news the gospel brings. The key distinction in this lesson is the distinction between *functional* and *formative* community. *Functional* community puts me at the center: I value relationships for how well they function to fulfill my needs and desires. (And if they don't function well or aren't "meeting my needs," I have no need for them.) *Formative* community puts God at the center: I value the relationships in my life as part of God's means to change me and re-form me to reflect his image. When I begin to see community as a means of spiritual formation, I see every struggle or problem I have in relationships as a "gospel opportunity"—a chance to believe the promises of the gospel more deeply and to rely on the Holy Spirit to change my heart and my life in the ways God desires.

NOTES:

HOW COMMUNITY SHAPES US IN THE GOSPEL

In the last lesson, we saw that we are created for community, redeemed for community, and transformed in community. We also observed that sin hinders community by making us self-centered and self-seeking. In this lesson, we want to see how community exposes our sin and unbelief, pushing us into a deeper dependence on the good news of the gospel. In other words, we want to move from a functional to a formative view of community.

As pragmatic people, we tend to have a *functional* view of community. Knowingly or unknowingly, we think of relationships in terms of what they do for *us*. Our friends give our lives meaning, keep us from being lonely and isolated, support us in hard times, celebrate with us, and help us accomplish goals. But what if our relationships had a more transcendent purpose? What if every friendship and interaction was intended by God to form us, shape us, and change us spiritually?

According to the Bible, that's exactly what God intends. Every relationship in our lives has a *formative* purpose. Consider these verses:

> **Acts 17:26–27:** "[God] made from one man every nation of mankind to live on all the face of the earth, having determined allotted periods and the boundaries of their dwelling place, that they should seek God. . . ."

25

Romans 11:36: "For from him and through him and to him are all things. To him be glory forever."

God has determined where we live and who lives near us. All things (including our relationships) are from him and for him. The community we're part of is not accidental. It's purposeful. God is using the people in our lives to form us, to shape us, to sanctify (purify) us. The Holy Spirit uses our struggles and failures in community to reveal our sin and show us our need for the heart and life change that Jesus' death and resurrection make possible.

Here's another way to say the same thing: On our own, we are relentlessly self-focused people. We want to be at the center of our lives and at the center of our relationships. That translates into a functional view of community that keeps ME at the center. The relationships in my life revolve around me and exist for me. But the *truth* is that God is the center of everything. "From him and through him and to him are all things." So every relationship in my life is ultimately about God. Every struggle, conflict, and broken relationship is an opportunity to worship God more deeply and be formed more fully into his image.

When I am the center:

- Every *conflict* leads to polarization: me vs. you. *I am the center, after all! How dare you not honor me as I deserve to be honored! We both need to change, but you need to change more.*
- I think *economically* about relationships: Anything I don't want to do becomes a cost, a demand, an "expense" of time and energy (because it takes me out of being the center). I may still do it because it's the "right thing to do," but I'll do it grudgingly and under compulsion, expecting repayment.
- I end up *using* others (both God and humans) to get what I really want (meaning, significance, security, productivity, etc.).

When God is at the center:

- Every *conflict* is an opportunity for gospel growth. It's not me vs. you; it's God, our heavenly Father, giving both of us an opportunity to see where we are trusting in something other than him and to turn to him in repentance so that we can grow as his image bearers. We tend to think that if relationships are difficult, something is wrong: "This just isn't working out." But if this is all part of God's redemptive plan, conflict is actually a mark of God's love. If you are dealing with a difficult person or in an awkward situation right now, cheer up! It means God loves you!

- I learn to think *graciously* about relationships. Anything I don't want to do becomes an opportunity to rely on God's grace and the Holy Spirit's power to love my neighbor as myself. Since God has loved me so generously by sending his Son (1 John 4:10), I can "lend, expecting nothing in return" (Luke 6:35).

- I can actually *love* other people instead of using them, because they're not a means to an end. God is the end. I'm satisfied in him and I'm able to reflect his grace and goodness to others.

So God graciously uses community to expose our sin and to invite us to believe the gospel and allow it to work change more deeply into our attitudes, motives, words, and actions. This week's exercise gives you an opportunity to see how this actually works by walking you through three questions:

- Identify a struggle you've had in community recently (a conflict, disagreement, misunderstanding, etc.).
- How does this struggle—or your response to it—expose your sin? What areas of unbelief, selfishness, or idolatry do you see in yourself?
- How does Jesus' death for our sins on the cross and his resurrection (redemption accomplished) speak to this struggle?
- How does the ongoing work of the Holy Spirit (redemption applied) free you to react differently in the midst of this struggle?

To help put flesh on this exercise, let me use a recent example from my life. For a few months, I've been holding a good friend at arm's length—not intentionally or consciously, but subtly and subconsciously. I thought things were fine. But he sensed the relational distance and brought it to my attention. He said I didn't seem relationally open, and he pointed to some specific conversations where I'd responded in defensive and self-protective ways.

My first response was to dismiss his concerns: "He's just upset because our relationship hasn't been working the way he wants lately." I wouldn't have said our relationship was great, but it wasn't all that bad either. It was functional, and I didn't want to spend time or energy fixing something that wasn't really that broken. I figured he would sort things out in time. But as the Holy Spirit reminded me that community is formative, I stepped back to take a more prayerful look at what God might be saying to me through my friend. Through prayer and conversation, I realized that I was acting out of deep unbelief. I *was* being self-protective. I *was* relationally distant. Other friends had abandoned me in painful ways in the past, and I was afraid of the same thing happening in this friendship. So I was remaining distant to protect myself from potential pain and hurt.

At the root, this was a gospel issue for me. My lack of trust in my friend was really a lack of trust in God. I didn't *believe* God would save me from pain or redeem whatever pain I might experience. I was really saying to God, "I'm a better Savior than Jesus. I don't trust *you* to save me, so I'll save myself."

Applying the gospel to my unbelief meant looking first to the *cross* to remember how Jesus actually *is* a better Savior than I am.

- At the cross, Jesus was abandoned by his closest friends and rejected by his Father so that I could be accepted. He experienced the worst and most painful rejection of all so that I have the surest and most lasting acceptance of all.
- At the cross, Jesus gave up being the center of his own world so that I could be restored to a living, breathing, growing relationship with God. I can trust him to be the center of my life now.
- At the cross, Jesus showed that he can be trusted to meet my deepest needs. I can be assured that God will love and care for me because he has already cared for me in the ultimate way, by sending his Son to die for me.

Applying the gospel to my unbelief means that I must not only look to the cross (where my redemption was *accomplished*), but also to the ongoing work of the Holy Spirit (who *applies* Jesus' redemption to my life and helps me change to be more like him).

- The Holy Spirit, who lives within me, is more powerful than my natural tendency toward self-protection. With his help, I can trust others and move toward them instead of away from them.
- "Perfect love casts out fear" (1 John 4:18). The Spirit helps me to know and feel God's love (Romans 8:14–16) so that I can live out of faith and not out of fear.
- By withholding myself, I am refusing to let the Spirit use me redemptively in the lives of others. God is not just redeeming me; he is redeeming his people, and he wants me to be a part of that work. By the Spirit, I can participate in God's redemptive work in others' lives.

So, in the recent situation with my friend, I first repented vertically (toward God). I acknowledged my unbelief, speaking honestly with God in prayer: "At some level, I really *don't* trust you to save me and redeem me. I've chosen to protect myself because of my unbelief. Please forgive me and let me rest in your salvation instead of trying to save myself." This sounds simple and trite as I write it, but in real life it rang with deep emotion, brokenness, and honesty. My repentance immediately turned to faith and worship as the Holy Spirit brought to mind specific Scripture passages to counter my unbelief. After I did the vertical work of repentance toward God, I met with my friend and asked his forgiveness. I told him how God had graced me with the gift of repentance, and I invited his help in my ongoing battle with self-protection. Instead of defensiveness and protection, I felt a deep gratitude for his friendship. And in church the following Sunday, my affections for Jesus were uniquely stirred. The gospel actually *felt* like good news for *me*.

The gospel is not just good news in general—it's good news for *you* and *your* particular struggles. And community is one of God's most gracious means to show you just how good the gospel is. You need community, not just because it's *functional,* but because it's *formative*. You can't become the person God wants you to be without it.

Lesson

EXERCISE

2

REDEMPTION IN COMMUNITY

This week's article reminds us that community is part of God's means to form us, shape us, and sanctify us as his children. The Holy Spirit uses our struggles and failures in community to reveal our sin and to show us our need for our hearts to be changed by the gospel's promises and power.

This is easy to agree with in the abstract, but it becomes genuinely life-changing—formative—when we see it working out in concrete situations. So take a few minutes to think through the following questions and then talk about them as a community.

1. Identify a struggle you've had recently as an individual in community. It could be a conflict, a disagreement, or a misunderstanding—or maybe even a tendency to avoid community.

2. How does this struggle—or your response to it—expose your sin? What areas of unbelief, selfishness, or idolatry do you see in yourself? (Remember that if the situation you have in mind is a conflict or disagreement, your tendency will be to focus on the other person's sin. And there may indeed *be* sin in the other person that needs to be dealt with! But for the purposes of this exercise, we're asking you to reflect on what the situation reveals about *your* heart.)

3. How does Jesus' death and resurrection (redemption *accomplished*) affect the way you respond to this struggle? Be specific.

How does his death and resurrection set you free and meet your deepest needs?

4. How does the ongoing work of the Holy Spirit (redemption *applied* to our hearts and lives) free you to react differently in the midst of this struggle? Again, be specific. How does the Spirit's presence and power free you to act redemptively; that is, to bring God's good out of a bad situation in joy, worship, and freedom?

Lesson

3

HOW THE GOSPEL SHAPES COMMUNITY

BIG IDEA

In the last lesson, we looked at the gospel through the lens of community. We saw that being in community exposes our sin and pushes us to believe the gospel more deeply; that is, to trust that what Jesus did for us has power to change us in all the ways we need. In this lesson, we want to look at community through the lens of the gospel. We want to explore how the gospel empowers and enables deeper community. We're not really introducing any new concepts; we're just coming at the same things from different angles. As a result of this lesson, you should see your group members begin to confront some of their barriers to deeper, more life-giving community.

NOTES:

COMMUNITY BARRIERS AND GOSPEL FREEDOM

In the last lesson, we saw that community exposes our sin and pushes us to trust more deeply in the power of Christ and the Holy Spirit to bring needed change to our lives. In this lesson, we want to explore how the gospel propels us into deeper community. By "deeper" community we mean community in which relationships are increasingly shaped by the good things that come from trusting Jesus and the promises of the gospel: things like a growing trust, openness, humility, service, teachability, and accountability in ways that reflect God's character and his intentions for human relationships. (We're still working out the same concepts, just coming at them from a different angle.)

Our goal is to apply the promises of the gospel to our lives as we read. So, as a starting point, pause and ask yourself this question: "What keeps me from experiencing deeper community?" Which of the following answers is closest to the truth?

- I'm too busy; I can't invest the time it requires.
- I'm happy with the relationships I have; I'm not looking for new ones.
- I have boundaries; don't push me.
- These people aren't like me; there's a limit to how "deep" we can go.
- Relationships overwhelm me; I don't have the capacity right now.

- If these people really knew me, I'm not sure they'd accept me.
- I don't want to inconvenience others by asking more of them.
- Something else; write it here. _____

_____

_____

Most of us have justified these barriers to community for so long that we don't see anything wrong with them. What's the big deal? The big deal is that, as we saw in Lesson 1, we are God's image bearers. So the depth of our community says something about God and his gospel! If we are content with shallow community, we are content to reflect a shallow and superficial image of who God is. Consider Jesus' words in Luke 6:32–33:

> "If you love those who love you, what benefit is that to you?
> For even sinners love those who love them. And if you do
> good to those who do good to you, what benefit is that to you?
> For even sinners do the same."

Jesus is saying that there is a "lowest common denominator" kind of community that's natural to humanity. Everyone loves people who are just like them. That's not surprising. That's not different. That's not God-exalting. But when Jesus binds a diverse people together in deep community, that is provocative. It elicits questions from the watching world. It testifies to something powerful (God and his gospel) at the core of our communal life. Our longing, then, is to form communities that entice the world to believe in Jesus: "May they all be one, just as you, Father, are in me, and I in you . . . so that the world may believe that you have sent me" (John 17:21).

In pursuit of that sort of community, let's go back to the barrier you identified a few paragraphs back and ask one simple question: What's underneath that?

Don't think "underneath" as in Sigmund Freud—we're not urging you to uncover some repressed memory from your childhood (unless you need to). Rather, think "underneath" as in a medical diagnosis: What's underneath that symptom? What's causing it? What core issues of unbelief does it reveal? Jesus said, "Out of the overflow of the heart the mouth speaks" (Luke 6:45 NIV). So these "barrier statements"—these objections to community—reveal even deeper barriers below the surface, in our hearts. Here are two categories to think through.

- **False Beliefs.** What false ideas (lies) about God, myself, and others am I believing as true?
- **False Sources of Hope/Trust.** What "false gods" am I hoping in, trusting in, relying on? What am I really counting on to make me happy, content, satisfied? (Here's a short list of common cultural gods: power, approval, control, comfort, respect, success, security.)

Here are two possible examples.

1. Community Barrier: "I have boundaries; don't push me."
- What's underneath that?
- False Beliefs:
    - About God: God's ways are overwhelming and difficult. I'll be more content if I do things my way instead of his way.
    - About myself: I always know what's best for me.
    - About others: They want something from me. They aren't out for my good.
- False Sources of Hope/Trust:
    - I'll be happy if I can prevent people from making demands on my time and energy. I'm trusting in the false god of *control*.

2. Community Barrier: "I don't want to inconvenience others."
- What's underneath that?
- False Beliefs:
    - About God: I'm probably an inconvenience to him too.
    - About myself: I'm not worth people's time and attention.
    - About others: They would probably reject or resent me if I "needed" them. I've really been burned before and I don't want to experience that sort of pain again.
- False Sources of Hope/Trust:
    - I'll be happy if people never see me as an inconvenience or feel like I'm making demands on them. I'm trusting in

the false god of *approval*. (I don't want to be perceived as a needy person.)

These are only two possible examples. They aren't exhaustive, and the lies and longings beneath your particular barrier might be completely different from the ones given here. The point is to help you see that the barriers and excuses that sabotage our attempts at community are actually gospel issues. They are symptoms of deeply held beliefs, objections, and longings that need to be changed by Jesus and what he has done for us.

So how do we build deeper community that reflects God more fully and displays his glory to the world more clearly? By believing the gospel more deeply. Here's a simple, biblical, four-step process to help you do that.

- **REPENT**. Turn *from* the lies and false gods you've identified. Ask God to show you how you've turned your back on him. Acknowledge that the sin and selfishness driving your unbelief are really a relational rejection of your heavenly Father, who loves you and wants the best for you.
- **BELIEVE**. Turn *to* Jesus and the good news of his gospel. Believe first of all that Jesus died for your sin and unbelief and receive his forgiveness anew. Believe secondly all the freeing truth of the gospel: that Jesus redeemed you *for* community and calls you *to* community, that he frees you to worship him (not yourself or others), that he gives you his Spirit to empower you for obedience. Remember that "belief" in the Bible is not just a cognitive word; it speaks of an intentional "dwelling on" all that is true of us in Christ and an ongoing dependence on him as we live in joyful obedience.
- **WORSHIP GOD**. Rejoice in the goodness, grace, and glory of God. Do this in prayer. Do this in community. Do this out loud. The more you treasure God, the more your soul will relax its grip on false gods. Worship is not just something you do on Sundays. It is an all-the-time, moment-by-moment response of your heart to who God is and what he has done for you.
- **LOVE OTHERS**. Now, by faith, start moving toward others to love them as you have been loved! The gospel frees you to love.

Gospel change is not an interior, navel-gazing sort of change; it is "faith expressing itself through love" (Galatians 5:6 NIV). Pursue deeper community. Enjoy people who are unlike you. Love those who are hard to love. And as you fail (which will happen a lot), start this process all over again!

This repentance and faith—this turning back to God and moving out in love—is not a one-time event. It's more like the basic step in a dance, a foundational pattern repeated over and over again, that creates a joyful, beautiful movement. This is how the gospel builds a deeper, more vibrant community.

The Scriptures call me to community. As I try to obey that call and move toward others, I encounter barriers that keep me from loving others as God has loved me. Those barriers reveal that I'm more needy, broken, and sinful than I thought! My natural response is to ignore, avoid, or excuse my brokenness. But Jesus invites me instead to acknowledge my sin and turn to him in repentance, faith, and worship. As I do this, I am changed. I begin to see how desperately I need to depend on God moment by moment (and this starts to feel good!). I start to trust that my Father loves me and wants the best for me. And I'm freed to love other people—my faith expresses itself in love for others.

Still, all this "I" and "me" talk is misleading. This isn't a process that happens alone as I pursue Jesus by myself. The whole thing happens in community. I need others to help me see my sin and point me to the gospel. And they need me to do the same for them. Being in community shines a light on my need for change. I'll need to repent, believe, worship, and love many, many, many more times in community than I would if I could just be left alone to pursue "Jesus and me."

So what does a healthy, vibrant Christian community look like? How does it avoid being shallow and superficial? It's honest. Struggling. Loving. Failing. Clinging to Jesus. Repenting to each other. Forgiving each other. Placing others ahead of ourselves. Helping point each other to the cross. This is the beautiful mess of gospel-centered community.

Lesson

3

EXERCISE

COMMUNAL PRAYER AND WORSHIP

The antidote to false belief and false sources of hope/trust is *worship*. It is by worshiping God in Spirit and truth that our hearts relax their grip on false beliefs and idols. So this week, as we close our study, we want to actually spend some time in prayer and worship together, focusing on what is true about God in a way that will loosen our grip on things that are false. We're going to practice actually *being* a gospel community instead of just talking about it.

Here's what we're going to do:

- Start by having someone read one of the following Scripture passages aloud:
  - Psalm 25
  - Psalm 103
  - Isaiah 55
  - Matthew 6:25–34
  - [any other passage that highlights God's goodness, grace, and power]
- Respond to the truth of the passage by praying out loud, worshiping God for what is true of him.
- If you've identified false beliefs and false gods that you're ready to turn from, then feel free to do that in prayer as well. You can confess your unbelief and idolatry and express your desire to worship and obey God above these things.

- If you're still sorting out the heart dynamics that hinder you from community, ask the Holy Spirit to shed light on those things.
- Do this exercise as a *community*, not as a gathering of individuals. Listen attentively to what others are saying. Pray with them and for them. Ask God to give you words. The Holy Spirit may lead you to pray or read specific things that will minister to others. You might even incorporate practices like holding hands, kneeling together, or laying hands on someone as you pray together for him. Are these things "awkward" in Western culture? Sure. But they're biblical, good, and appropriate. And they help confront our barriers to community.

The goal of this exercise is to turn our hearts toward God and awaken deeper love for him, together.

Are you ready? Let's begin.

Lesson

4

FAITH WORKING THROUGH LOVE

BIG IDEA

In the first three lessons of this study, we've laid a foundation for gospel-centered community. We've seen that God himself is in community and that he made us in his image as communal beings. We've seen that the fall has turned us in on ourselves, causing us to sabotage meaningful relationships with others through our unbelief and idolatry. And we've seen how Jesus redeems us, restores our capacity for community, and calls us into his new community (the church), the context for our ongoing transformation. Now we come to a "hinge point" in the study—the concept of "faith working through love" (Galatians 5:6). We will never love one another as God intends unless we understand how faith in the work of Christ provides the foundation and the motivation for love. This lesson establishes a core principle that we'll return to in Lessons 5 through 9.

NOTES:

MAKING IT COUNT

In the past three lessons, we've tried to lay the foundation for a gospel-centered community. We've seen that God himself is in community, and that he made us in his image as communal beings. We've seen that the fall has turned us in on ourselves, causing us to sabotage relationships through our unbelief and idolatry. And we've seen how Jesus redeems us, restores our capacity for community, and calls us into his new community (the church), the context for our ongoing transformation. We've seen how our failures in community drive us more deeply into the gospel, and how the good news of the gospel frees us for richer and more life-giving community.

The current lesson is a hinge point in this study. In Lessons 5 through 9, we're going to examine some of the defining marks or characteristics of a biblical community—things like humility, honesty, and forgiveness. In other words, we're going to consider what our communities *should* look like. The Bible is not vague on this matter; it's full of teaching about how God's people *should* relate to one another.

But before we can get to the *shoulds*—the imperatives—of gospel-centered community, we have to get clear on how the gospel empowers us to obey. Otherwise, God's ideals for community will overwhelm us, driving us to despair and defeat.

Consider these exhortations:

- "Love one another with brotherly affection; outdo one another in showing honor" (Romans 12:10*)*.

- "Do not let any unwholesome talk come out of your mouths, but only what is helpful for building others up according to their needs, that it may benefit those who listen" (Ephesians 4:29 NIV).
- "Be kind to one another, tenderhearted, forgiving one another, as God in Christ forgave you" (Ephesians 4:32).
- "Let every person be quick to hear, slow to speak, slow to anger" (James 1:19).

Think for a minute about how difficult it is to obey these commands—not in the abstract, but with *actual people* you know. *That* guy or *that* girl. Every time. With the right attitudes and motives. Are you beginning to feel the tension? Where can we find the power to live up to this ideal?

When confronted with these kinds of demands and expectations, we tend to respond in one of two ways:

- **Resolution.** "I'm going to do that." I have a high view of my willpower and my moral ability. If I think I'm succeeding, I will quickly become self-righteous: "I did this; why can't others?"
- **Resignation.** "There's no way I can do that. I might as well not even try." I have a faulty view of God and his standard: it's not even worth trying if it seems beyond me or if it will reveal my faults and failures. This is also a subtle form of self-righteousness: "I shouldn't have to keep the rules."

Both resolution and resignation are alive and well on the pages of Scripture. The Pharisees and religious leaders were masters of resolution and the self-righteousness that accompanies it. In one of his teachings, Jesus mocks the way a Pharisee might pray: "God, I thank you that I am not like other men. . . . I fast twice a week; I give tithes of all that I get" (Luke 18:11–12). On the other hand, the irreligious Gentiles tended toward resignation. They flaunted their "freedom" from God's law: "They have become callous and have given themselves up to sensuality, greedy to practice every kind of impurity" (Ephesians 4:19). The difference between the two groups was evident in their approach to circumcision.

Circumcision was a rite God had commanded in the Old Testament to physically mark his covenant with his people (see Genesis 17:1–14). The Jewish Christians prided themselves on their obedience to this command. They even argued that Gentile converts to Christianity should be circumcised. But the Gentiles enjoyed their freedom from this practice. For this reason, circumcision became one of the most contentious issues in the early church.

Circumcision might seem like a strange issue to fight about. But it's really not so strange when you think about it. It was a good thing, given by God, that had become a boundary marker—a way of determining who was "really spiritual" and who wasn't. We have all sorts of similar markers in our day: church attendance, small group involvement, external appearance (clothes and "look"), political views, language, preferred Bible translation. Scrupulous people identify themselves by these things. Skeptical people identify themselves by their "freedom" from these things. But either way, we're not identifying ourselves by Jesus. And that's a problem!

The book of Galatians was written to a church rife with conflict over the issue of circumcision. After spending four chapters applying the truth of the gospel to the question, the apostle Paul summed the matter up succinctly in one verse: "For in Christ Jesus, neither circumcision nor uncircumcision counts for anything, but only faith working through love" (Galatians 5:6).

In Christ Jesus. That's the gospel. We are united with Jesus through faith: his life is credited to us, his death is in our place, his resurrection is our "newness of life" (Romans 6:4). When we rest in the good news that God saves us through our faith in Christ, we increasingly understand our new identity "in Christ Jesus." This changes everything about how we live. Circumcision and uncircumcision don't "count" anymore. They lose their value and meaning as marks that identify the people who belong to God. The only thing that does that now—and the thing that empowers our new life in community—is faith working through love.

Notice the precision of this phrase, "faith working through love." It's not faith by itself. It's not love by itself. It's not resolution (trying really hard to love) or resignation (falling back on my "faith" to excuse my lack of love). It's *faith working through love*. We can deduce at least two principles about faith and love from this phrase.

- Where there is no faith, there can be no real love. Faith is the energy that empowers love.
- Where there is no love, there is no real faith. The absence of faith can be discerned most clearly through the absence of love.

Applying these principles to our life in community, we see that:

- We often discover our *failure of faith* only when we examine the details of a particular situation where we have *failed to love*. The lack of love always indicates unbelief, or a lack of faith.
- We can own up to our *lack of love* only when we are appropriating the truth of the gospel into our own lives—that is, *resting by faith* in Christ's righteousness and God's love for us.

What counts is faith working through love. This is how the gospel empowers us to actually *obey* God's commands for Christian community. As we fail to meet God's standards for community (for example, as we judge others, isolate ourselves, avoid difficult people, etc.), we see our *lack of love* and are forced to confront our *lack of faith* (our fundamental unbelief in the good news of the gospel). Our love problem is really a faith problem. As we rest more fully in Christ's righteousness and God's love for us, we are empowered by the Holy Spirit to love others as God has loved us. Our faith works itself out in love.

This simple truth is the foundation of gospel-centered community, and it's a reality we'll return to over and over again in the rest of this study. Our lack of love always reveals a lack of faith—a "gospel disconnect." So the way to build deeper community (love) is to delight in the gospel more fully (faith). As we dwell on all we have received in Jesus and invite the Holy Spirit to work it down deep into the fabric of our hearts and lives, we'll be able to admit our lack of love, receive God's grace, and move toward others as God has moved toward us.

FAITH WORKING THROUGH LOVE

"For in Christ Jesus neither circumcision nor uncircumcision counts for anything, but only faith working through love" (Galatians 5:6).

The goal of this exercise is to take the basic biblical command of "faith working through love" and apply it practically in your everyday existence. Do this exercise in community. Talk honestly with one another. "You can't see your own face"—you need others to help you see yourself rightly. So, as a group, walk through the steps below one at a time. Then close by praying together.

1. Below are some specific ways the Bible commands us to love one another. Pick the one that challenges you most.

   - "Do not let any unwholesome talk come out of your mouths, but only what is helpful for building others up according to their needs . . . " (Ephesians 4:29 NIV).
   - "Let every person be quick to hear, slow to speak, slow to anger" (James 1:19).
   - "Admonish the idle, encourage the fainthearted, help the weak, be patient with all" (1 Thessalonians 5:14).
   - "Accept one another, then, just as Christ accepted you, in order to bring praise to God" (Romans 15:7 NIV).
   - "I appeal to you, brothers, by the name of our Lord Jesus Christ, that all of you agree and that there be no divisions among you" (1 Corinthians 1:10).

2. As you seek to obey this command, do you tend toward *resolution* ("I'm going to make this happen!") or *resignation* ("I have a hard time in this area. Maybe I'll just give up.")?

3. What would "faith working through love" look like in this area?

- How does your failure in this area—your lack of love—reveal a lack of faith? Where is there unbelief in your heart? What "good news" about God and his grace are you not really believing? (This is where we really need to invite others to speak into our lives. We want to help each other articulate specific areas of unbelief and get below the surface <u>by sharing our own relevant stories</u>. If we could figure things out on our own, then what's the point of the exercise? We need others to tell us what they see in us.)

- How might a deeper confidence and joy in God's love, in Christ's righteousness, and in the Holy Spirit's presence work itself out in greater obedience to this command?

Finally, close the group by praying out loud together. Those who are willing can confess their unbelief and ask the Holy Spirit to convince them more deeply of the truth of the gospel so that they can more freely love others.

SAMPLE RESPONSES

If you are having a hard time knowing how to respond to the exercise, here are two examples of what good answers might look like.

DAVE

Dave finds it hard to commit to any one thing for long. Nothing seems to really grab his attention—not even a relationship that requires more than a few weeks or months of commitment. His attendance at your community group is pretty haphazard though probably the most consistent thing he does.

When you talked with Dave about this, his response was, "I just don't like being tied down. If I do something because I want to, then I like it and it's good. But when I feel like I'm being forced to do something, it feels artificial. I don't want to have to pretend with people who should love me as I am."

JAN

Jan is a mom with three children and a husband with a busy career. Every day is a whirlwind for her as she works tirelessly to invest in her kids' lives and activities. She generally seems "put together," arriving for group on time, ready to go, but she's not always the friendliest person.

1. Below are some specific ways the Bible commands us to love one another. Pick the one that challenges you most.

- "I appeal to you, brothers, by the name of our Lord Jesus Christ, that all of you agree and that there be no divisions among you" (1 Corinthians 1:10).
  Dave's answer: "I chose the 1 Corinthians passage because I feel like sometimes I create divisions in the group. When you ask me to take a turn lining up refreshments or leading our prayer time, I don't really want to say, 'Yes, you can count on me.' But when I don't say that, I feel a lot of tension with you. I'm not being argumentative or trying to be divisive, but I really get the sense that it's not okay for 'me to be me.'"

- "Admonish the idle, encourage the fainthearted, help the weak, be patient with all" (1 Thessalonians 5:14).
  Jan's answer: "The last part of the verse from Thessalonians really grabbed me, 'be patient with all.' I'm so not patient. Not just here, but in every area of my life. I have so much to do; I don't have the time to be patient. I need people to be ready to go and to stay on track or my whole world falls apart. So when someone in the group shows up late or forgot it was their week to get the snacks, I just think, 'What is wrong with you! My life is way harder than yours, but I'm here and ready to go. You need to take things more seriously.'"

2. As you seek to obey this command, do you tend toward **resolution** ("I'm going to make this happen!") or **resignation** ("I have a hard time in this area. Maybe I'll just give up.")?

> **Dave's** answer: "I'd like to say I struggle with resignation, but I'm not sure I struggle all that much. I just figure, 'This is how I am,' and go with it. The few times when some of you have told me that I'm not taking my responsibility to the group seriously, I've tried to improve a little bit. But really, I know I won't get better, so I don't try all that hard."

> **Jan's** answer: "I didn't even know 'resignation' was a possibility! I'm a 'I'm going to make this happen' person. And I expect others to be the same way, especially my kids and my husband. I can let things slide when things don't happen, but not if you didn't try your very best."

3. What would "faith working through love" look like in this area?

> - How does your failure in this area—your lack of love—reveal a lack of faith? Where is there unbelief in your heart? What "good news" about God and his grace are you not really believing?
> **Dave's** answer: "Well, I never thought about my not wanting to be committed as a lack of love! I just assumed that we should all make allowances for each other. I guess I can admit that my lack of commitment to all of you is actually unloving because it's selfish on my part. I really just want to do what is easy for me without thinking about anyone else. So I guess that isn't very loving.

> **"I think at s**ome level I don't believe that God will really take care of me and fill me up. That's why I want to keep my options open. If I don't feel like something will be enjoyable, I don't want to do it. I guess this 'I'll only do what I feel like' mentality is an idol—I don't find Jesus completely satisfying. I need the freedom to pursue the next thing that will make me feel complete. Without that freedom, I don't trust Jesus to be enough for me."

> **Jan's** answer: "I can be chilly with people. I'm not all rah-rah about the latest movie or book because I don't have time for

those things. But I didn't really think of that as being 'unloving' to others. Well, maybe I did a bit, especially when I found myself thinking, 'You have no idea how easy your life is compared to mine.'

"What I'm starting to see is that when I'm so gung-ho on seeing that my agenda gets pursued, I tend to leave people in the dust. I feel like that's how God treats me: if I work hard to be a good mom and wife, if my house is all put together, if I'm doing the right things, then God is happy with me. But if I'm running behind and don't have my devotions, it feels like God is saying, "Jan, if you loved me you wouldn't be so disorganized and miss your time with me. It's okay, but I want you to do better." Maybe you've seen me treat others that way."

- How might a deeper confidence and joy in God's love, in Christ's righteousness, and in the Holy Spirit's presence work itself out in greater obedience to this command?

  Dave's answer: "I guess if I was thinking through the article, neither 'obeying the rules about being committed to the group' nor 'disobeying the rules about being committed to the group' is really the issue. The issue is: am I loving the people God has called me to love or not? So when I'm feeling like I'd really rather do something else—going to a movie instead of being here or hanging out with other friends—I probably need to take some time to see what Christ is offering me. He offers me the satisfaction of being known and loved by him completely; finding freedom from having to satisfy myself and remembering that he can make me feel fulfilled in ways that other things just can't; reminding me that part of how he meets my needs is through all of you and part of the way he meets your needs is through me. When I think of things that way, it does make me want to be present to catch up with you and find out how God has been working in your life."

  Jan's answer: "I want to be organized and focused, but I don't want to be someone who loves those things more than she loves other people. I suppose what it comes down to is that if I could really believe God loved me—even though I am a mess and not doing all the things I know I should do—I'd look at life differently. Instead of comparing myself with others or wanting everyone to know how hard I have it, I think I could rest in him more, really look to what he's already done for my identity and security instead of what I need to do. That would change the way I think about my to-do list and help me to take time to love people more."

SECTION 2:
THE FRUIT OF GOSPEL-CENTERED COMMUNITY

5

A JOYFUL COMMUNITY

BIG IDEA

In the last lesson, we examined the concept of "faith working through love" (Galatians 5:6). We saw that our lack of love always reveals a lack of faith—a "gospel disconnect." We said that this idea of faith working through love is a "hinge point" in the study and a core principle we'll return to over and over again. In this lesson, we begin to look at some of the characteristic marks of gospel-centered community. The first—and perhaps the most important—is joy. If joy is missing from Christian community, it's a clear indication that something is amiss in our understanding of the gospel. This lesson will help us understand why the relationship between justification and sanctification is crucial to experiencing joy in Christ.

NOTES:

A JOYFUL COMMUNITY

One of the defining characteristics of a gospel-centered community is JOY.

If we have believed the good news of the gospel, and if we are experiencing the ongoing work of the Holy Spirit through repentance and faith, we *will* be a joyful people. There's no way around it! Joy is one of the by-products of knowing Jesus as Savior and Lord. "The fruit of the Spirit is . . . joy" (Galatians 5:22).

Notice how Scripture consistently describes joy as a consequence of believing the gospel:

> **1 Peter 1:8–9**: "Though you have not seen him, you love him. Though you do not now see him, you *believe* in him and *rejoice* with *joy* that is inexpressible and filled with glory, obtaining the outcome of your faith, the salvation of your souls."

> **Romans 15:13:** "May the God of hope fill you with all *joy* and peace *in believing*, so that by the power of the Holy Spirit you may abound in hope."

> **Acts 13:48, 52:** "And when the Gentiles heard this, they began rejoicing and glorifying the word of the Lord, and as many as were appointed to eternal life *believed*. . . . And the disciples were filled with *joy* and with the Holy Spirit."

1 Thessalonians 1:5–6 (NASB): "Our *gospel* did not come to you in word only, but also in power and in the Holy Spirit and with full conviction. . . . You also became imitators of us and of the Lord, having *received* the word in much tribulation with the *joy* of the Holy Spirit."

The conclusion is clear: God's people ought to be consistently, recognizably, resolutely joyful.

So take a moment and think about yourself. Are you a joyful person? Do people see you that way? Now think about your church or community group. Is it marked by radical joy? Would outsiders spending time among you comment on the deep joy they see in your community?

Many of us would have to admit that joy isn't always the defining characteristic of our souls or of our communities. And we don't always recognize that as a significant problem. If our churches aren't biblically literate, or if they aren't missionally effective, making disciples, or if they aren't growing, *those* are issues we think are worth talking about. But a lack of joy? What's the big deal?

Allow Martyn Lloyd-Jones, an influential twentieth-century British preacher, to answer that question.

> Christian people too often seem to be perpetually in the doldrums and too often give this appearance of unhappiness and of lack of freedom and absence of joy. There is no question at all but that this is the main reason why large numbers of people have ceased to be interested in Christianity. . . . In a world where everything has gone so sadly astray, we should be standing out as men and women apart, people characterized by a fundamental joy!*

---

* D. Martyn Lloyd-Jones, *Spiritual Depression: Its Causes and Cures* (Grand Rapids: Eerdmans, 1965), 12, 23.

Our lack of joy is a missional issue. It's a gospel issue. For the glory of God, for the good of others, and for the cause of the gospel, we must relentlessly pursue joy. But how? How do we become more joyful?

In the last lesson, we saw that a lack of love always reveals a lack of faith. The same is true for a lack of joy. If we lack joy, our real problem is unbelief. We are not fully trusting and resting in Jesus and what he accomplished for us in his death and resurrection. Joy comes from be-lieving: "May the God of hope fill you with all joy and peace in [or *by*] believing" (Romans 15:13).

So what is the "belief problem" beneath our lack of joy? Quite commonly, the problem is that we've confused *justification* and *sanctification*.

Justification is the theological term that refers to God's once-for-all dec-laration of forgiveness and pardon (and more). It's a legal term, so it might help to picture a heavenly courtroom. God is the Judge and you stand before him guilty, on trial for your sins. But because of your faith in Christ and his death on the cross on your behalf, the gavel falls and God pronounces you "not guilty." You are forgiven, freed, and pardoned! The "guilty" verdict for your sin is transferred to Jesus. But that's not all. Jesus' record of perfect righteousness is also credited to *you*. So you're not just forgiven; you're declared righteous in Christ! This is a once-for-all, completed judicial transaction that happens the moment you trust in Jesus: "Since we have been justified by faith [past-tense, once-and-for-all], we [now] have peace with God" (Romans 5:1).

Sanctification is the theological term that refers to our ongoing trans-formation into Christlikeness. It's a progressive journey toward holi-ness that continues throughout our lives. Sometimes it proceeds at a dramatic and breathtaking pace. Other times it's slow and methodical. But it's always happening, because God is faithful: "He who began a good work in you will carry it on to completion until the day of Christ Jesus" (Philippians 1:6 NIV). While justification is a one-time act of God, sanc-tification is an ongoing process that requires our cooperation: "Present your members [of your body] as slaves to righteousness, leading to sanctification" (Romans 6:19).

Here's the great mistake that often steals our joy: our confidence in our *justification* tends to be based on our *sanctification*. In other words, unless we're really "doing well" in holiness and obedience, we doubt whether we're truly forgiven by God and credited with Christ's righteousness. When we're struggling in the sanctification process, plagued by the same sins over and over again, when we can't seem to "get our act together" spiritually, we question whether God could really accept and love us. Sometimes we wonder if we're even Christians at all. We live in defeat, despair, and discouragement.

Do you see this pattern in yourself? Do you see it in Christians around you?

When our confidence in our justification is based on our sanctification, what we're really doing is falling into self-righteousness. It doesn't *feel* that way because, after all, we don't *feel* righteous! But think about it: If our lack of sanctification (our lack of day-to-day righteousness) causes us to doubt God's love and acceptance, then whose righteousness are we actually relying on? Our own! *This* is the reason we lack joy. *This* is the reason we're "spiritually depressed." We're trusting in ourselves! (Let's face it, who *wouldn't* be depressed?)

So how do we experience lasting joy? By believing the truth of justification by faith. We must start every day claiming the great biblical promises of justification: I have peace with God (Romans 5:1). Jesus bore my sins in his body on the cross (1 Peter 2:24). God has credited Jesus' righteousness to me by faith (Romans 4:5). It is finished (John 19:30). How great these truths are! How rich and joyful these realities are! I don't contribute a single thing to my justification. My sanctification—or lack of it—changes nothing. It's Jesus' righteousness that guarantees my acceptance before God. "Nothing in my hand I bring, simply to thy cross I cling," says an old hymn.** Jesus' righteousness is the ONLY righteousness I need.

Relying completely on justification by faith—Christ's work on my behalf—is crucial to deep and abiding joy. When my sanctification is slow

---

** "Rock of Ages," Augustus M. Toplady, 1776.

and my struggles against sin are intense, I'm still joyful because Jesus is my righteousness! When my sanctification is rapid and I'm experiencing victory over sin, I'm joyful because Jesus is my righteousness! Even my striving for sanctification is permeated by joy because I'm motivated by love (knowing I already have God's favor) instead of fear (trying to earn God's favor). This discipline of resting in my justification by faith is a constant process of reorientation and reminding. It's ongoing. It's daily. It requires me to hear the Spirit's conviction when I am not believing or obeying. (We'll be doing an exercise to help us learn how to do this moment by moment.)

We have been using a lot of "I" language in this lesson because justification must be experienced individually before it can be celebrated communally. But the point is this: a gospel-centered community will be a community of radical joy. So take some time together to assess and evaluate your community. Is it joyful—persistently, demonstrably, and resolutely joyful? If not, where does the truth of justification by faith need to sink in more deeply? How can you help each other grow in faith—and therefore in joy?

5

GROWING IN JOY

> It may sound paradoxical . . . but you must be made miserable before you can know true Christian joy. Indeed the real trouble with the miserable Christian is that he has never been truly made miserable because of conviction of sin. He has bypassed the essential preliminary to joy. —Martyn Lloyd-Jones, *Spiritual Depression: It's Causes and Cures*

> Question: What must you know to live and die in the joy of [gospel] comfort? Answer: Three things: first, how great my sin and misery are; second, how I am set free from all my sins and misery; third, how I am to thank God for such deliverance. —*The Heidelberg Catechism,* Question 2

If, as this week's article states, joy comes from basing our sanctification on our justification, then growing in joy requires us to learn how to live out of our justification on a daily basis. Just like oxygen, we need to be breathing in the truth of the gospel constantly. We can't "get a little Jesus" during our small group time or Sunday worship and live off that for the rest of the week any more than we could take one big breath in the morning and then say, "I'm good. I've got my daily supply of oxygen."

This week's exercise is designed to help us start learning how to regularly (constantly!) breathe in the good news of the gospel. Doing this allows us to relate to God and others based on what Christ has already accomplished for us instead of how well we are "performing." It is this identity—people who are God's beloved children and now have the same record of righteousness that Jesus has—that is the foundation for all of our obedience. As we learn to live out our new identity, we'll also begin to change in other ways—what we do, what we love, what we desire, how we live.

But as the quotes above point out, we need to start this process by seeing where our unbelief is at work, robbing us of the joy that comes from resting in Christ. Even though we're going to do this exercise together as a group, it's really something we all need to learn to do many, many times each day. In fact, you may want to write out a few key words (e.g., seeing my sin, set free by the cross, thanking God in love) that will remind you of each of these stages. Post that note on your computer at work, in your car, or on a mirror at home. Seeing it will remind you that we need Jesus—and the message of his good news—just like we need air.

STEP ONE: SEEING OUR SIN

- Pick an area where you're struggling right now in sanctification. It could be a poor prayer life, a failure to love others, a persistent character flaw, etc.
- How is your failure in this area causing you to *feel* toward God? Do you feel distant from him? Discouraged? Defeated? Not very useful? Different people will feel different things. Describe how you feel toward God as you think about your failure to faithfully obey him.
- Now, think about those same feelings in terms of *unbelief*. What are you *not* believing about the gospel and, specifically, about justification? How do your feelings reveal that you are trusting in your own performance instead of resting in Christ's accomplishments for you?

STEP TWO: REMEMBERING AND RECEIVING WHAT WE HAVE IN CHRIST

Now, practice getting your eyes off yourself and onto Christ by remembering and receiving the great promises of justification by faith. Here are three categories to think through.

1. **Justification (Negative):** Though I am a sinner, God has forgiven all my sins—past, present, and future—because of what Christ did for me. I am no longer under condemnation. I don't have to pay for my sins doing penance or work my way back into God's favor. Romans 8:1: "There is therefore now no condemnation for those who are in Christ Jesus."

2. **Justification (Positive):** Despite my ongoing struggles with sin, Jesus' righteousness and obedience have been credited to me. His "rightness" is now mine. When God looks at me, he doesn't see my sin; he sees Jesus' righteousness. 2 Corinthians 5:21 (NASB): "He made Him who knew no sin to be sin on our behalf, so that we might become the righteousness of God in Him."

3. **Adoption:** God doesn't just forgive me; he adopts me as his beloved child. My identity is not "forgiven sinner" but "beloved child of my heavenly Father." Galatians 4:4–6: "But when the fullness of time had come, God sent forth his Son, born of woman, born under the law, to redeem those who were under the law, so that we might receive adoption as sons. And because you are sons, God has sent the Spirit of his Son into our hearts, crying, 'Abba! Father!'"

Which of these promises speaks most directly to your area of unbelief identified in Step One?

STEP THREE: RESPONDING IN JOYFUL GRATITUDE

- Finally, ask: "If I really believed the truth of justification by faith, what would I be doing (or feeling, or thinking) differently?" The benefits we have in Christ don't just make us feel better about our relationship with God; they also draw us to love others more, to respond to God in gratitude and obedience, and to repent and turn from harmful, sinful things.

- Spend some time sharing some things you are grateful for and joyful about as a result of these realities. Doing this together makes gratitude and joy contagious. Don't turn this third step into introspective navel-gazing. The point is to see that faith—resting in Christ's righteousness—brings joy! Notice that we're not asking, "What *should* you be doing differently?" We're asking, "How *would* faith work itself out in love (and joy)?"

As you close this exercise, spend a few moments worshiping "in the moment"—that is, praying short prayers thanking God for the great gift of justification by faith. As you learn to "breathe in the good news of the gospel" many times each day, praying short worshipful prayers like this will help you rejoice in Christ moment by moment.

Lesson

6

A HUMBLE COMMUNITY

BIG IDEA

One mark of a gospel-centered community is humility. All of us want to be part of a community where pride and ego are put to death and selfless-ness and service are brought to life. That kind of community exalts God and blesses humanity. So what hinders that sort of community? Pride, of course. But pride is one of those abstract concepts that we talk about vaguely yet rarely think about in particular. To grow in humility, we need to identify the ways pride manifests itself in our lives and we need to put pride to death by looking to Jesus as our example and experiencing his grace personally. This lesson seeks to help you understand biblical humility, become a more humble person, and shape a more humble community that is eager to serve.

NOTES:

A HUMBLE COMMUNITY

Before her death in 1997, Mother Teresa spent her life serving the poor in the slums of Calcutta. Her mission, in her own words, was to serve "the hungry, the naked, the homeless, the crippled, the blind, the lepers, all those people who feel unwanted, unloved, uncared for throughout society, people that have become a burden to the society and are shunned by everyone."*

Mother Teresa never sought fame or power. And yet, in an odd way, she had both. She won the Nobel Peace Prize. She inspired millions. She influenced presidents and kings. She is one of the most admired and revered humanitarians in recent history.

We may argue about her politics or disagree with her religious convictions, but all of us feel a desire to honor a person like Mother Teresa. Why? Because she considered other people's needs above her own. Not just in her ideology, but in her practice.

All of us want to be part of a community where people consider the needs of others and take action to meet them—a community where pride and ego are put to death and selflessness and service are brought to life. This is just the kind of community the Bible urges us toward: "Do nothing from selfishness or empty conceit, but with humility of mind regard

---

*   Kathryn Spink, *Mother Teresa: A Complete Authorized Biography* (New York: HarperCollins, 1997), 18–21.

one another as more important than yourselves; do not merely look out for your own personal interests, but also for the interests of others" (Philippians 2:3–4 NASB).

Notice that the key to servanthood is "humility of mind." If we want a more serving community, we must cultivate humility. In other words, our lack of service to others is primarily because we lack humility. John Stott wrote, "At every stage of our Christian development and in every sphere of our Christian discipleship, pride is the greatest enemy and humility our greatest friend." The table below contrasts the consumer and the servant.

A CONSUMER	A SERVANT
"What's in it for me?"	"How can I serve others?"
"Who's going to relate to me and meet my needs?"	"Who can I relate to and whose needs can I meet?"
Critical of the community's faults and weaknesses	Looking for God's grace at work in the community
Gravitates toward people who have something to offer	Recognizes the diversity of gifts in the body
Uses others for personal gain	Empowers others for the good of the kingdom

The essence of pride is *self-concern*. It may manifest itself as arrogance and boasting or as self-protection and fear of people—but it's pride either way and it kills community. We have all been in a community where everyone seems to enjoy each other, but below the surface all are preoccupied with self: worried about how they are perceived by others, anxious about their needs, desperate for attention, insecure or self-righteous as they compare themselves with others, and the like. All forms of self-concern manifest themselves in a lack of love for others. We become consumers instead of servants. Such self-absorption can turn an entire community in on itself, concerned only about those within it and indifferent to the staggering needs of the world beyond it.

Our consumerism is rooted in a lack of faith. We are worried about what others think because we are not convinced that God delights in us (Psalm 149:4). We are anxious because we do not believe God will meet our needs (Matthew 6:32). We vie for attention because we do not think God rewards what is done in secret (Matthew 6:6). We compare ourselves to others because we forget that Jesus is our righteousness (1 Corinthians 1:30). A consumer is self-seeking because he is preoccupied with building his own kingdom in order to meet his own needs. Jesus calls us to just the opposite: "Seek first the kingdom of God and his righteousness, and all these things will be added to you" (Matthew 6:33).

Those who trust God to meet their needs are free to consider the needs of others. They discover this gospel paradox: As long as I'm looking to get my needs met, I will never get my needs met. But when I begin to meet the needs of others—when I begin to live for them instead of for myself—I find that God graciously takes care of my needs in the process.

The grace of God turns us into servants. Rather than demanding that we be served, we joyfully lay down our rights and seek to serve God and others. But it begins with "humility of mind," which we only get by looking to Jesus and understanding more deeply the gospel's implications for our lives. Paul shows us how in Philippians 2.

Right after his exhortation to consider others more important than ourselves, he said, "Have this mind among yourselves, which is yours in Christ Jesus, who, though he was in the form of God, did not count equality with God a thing to be grasped, but emptied himself, by taking the form of a servant, being born in the likeness of men" (Philippians 2:5–7).

Jesus serves as our example of the ultimate servant. He had a right to be served simply because he is God, but rather than claim that right, Jesus became flesh in the form of a humble servant. "The Son of Man came not to be served, but to serve, and to give his life as a ransom for many" (Mark 10:45).

Jesus serves us personally so that we can experience his grace. But often we aren't comfortable with a God who serves us. Instead, selfishly (and ironically), we want to serve God *so that* we can demand something in return. We want a transaction: Because I've done X for God, God should do Y for me. But when we allow Jesus to serve us, when we accept his grace instead of insisting on repaying him, we are humbled. This is how Paul could say, "Christ Jesus came into the world to save sinners, of whom I am the foremost. But I received mercy for this reason, that in me, as the foremost, Jesus Christ might display his perfect patience as an example to those who were to believe in him for eternal life" (1 Timothy 1:15–16).

Jesus transforms us from selfish consumers to faithful servants. Through the gospel, we become "bond-servants" of Christ—free persons who willingly become servants out of gratitude and honor to our master. "This is how one should regard us, as servants of Christ and stewards of the mysteries of God" (1 Corinthians 4:1). As bond-servants of Christ, we live to serve others, for Jesus' sake and for God's glory. "For we do not preach ourselves, but Jesus Christ as Lord, and ourselves as your servants for Jesus' sake" (2 Corinthians 4:5 NIV). As this penetrates our hearts, we will be eager to bless not just each other, but the world around us as well.

Humility of mind involves more than the intellect. God's grace toward us in Christ needs to get down deep into our hearts in order to change us. We need to acknowledge our resistance to grace—our reluctance to be served by Jesus. We need to "give up" and allow him to serve us in the ways we so desperately need. And we need to reflect on his gracious humility toward us so that our hearts are softened and changed. Then we will find ourselves increasingly joyful and selfless as we delight in serving him by serving others in our community and reaching beyond ourselves to serve those who do not yet know Jesus.

PRIDE AND PREJUDICE

We commonly think of pride only as arrogance or haughtiness. But the essence of pride is **self-concern,** which can manifest itself offensively (as arrogance) or defensively (as fear). The two lists below show characteristics of arrogant pride and fearful pride. Mark the two or three characteristics you see reflected most often in your life. (***Note:*** This isn't an either/or exercise. Most people will display tendencies from both lists.)

CHARACTERISTICS OF ARROGANT PRIDE

- I must be in control.
- I see most issues as black and white and tend to view people as either for me or against me.
- I am threatened by people with legitimate differences. I avoid disagreement or critique.
- I am often insensitive; I don't take other people's feelings into account.
- I tend to be closed-minded and committed to my own way of seeing things.
- I see other gifted, competent people as competition.
- I can be hypercritical of others.
- I lack self-awareness. I have a hard time seeing or admitting my sins, errors, and faults.
- I like to do things myself; I don't delegate significant responsibilities to others.
- I long to be respected by everyone.

CHARACTERISTICS OF FEARFUL PRIDE

- I avoid leadership; I'm hesitant to take charge.
- I see all issues as shades of gray. I'm reluctant to fight for anything.
- I'm paralyzed by people with legitimate differences. I spend lots of time and energy thinking about or responding to disagreement and critique.
- I'm overly sensitive; I don't want to hurt anyone's feelings.
- I'm overly welcoming of new ideas and viewpoints. I don't have many strong convictions or opinions.
- I see other gifted, competent people as threats.
- I am rarely critical of others—even when I should be.
- I lack self-confidence; I am often paralyzed by an awareness of my sins, errors, and faults.
- I want everybody to have a voice in every decision.
- I long to be liked by everyone.

Now, look back at the characteristics you've identified and consider the following questions:

- What elements of self-concern are present in the tendencies you identified? (How are these things ultimately about *you*, not others?)
- How do these tendencies hinder you from glorifying God and serving others?
- How does the gospel address this lack of humility and love? (Be as specific as possible.)
- What will repentance and faith look like for you in this area?

Now, consider how we function together as a group. Do you see evidence of a consumer orientation instead of a servant's heart? Do we focus on our neediness to the point that we have no energy for others? Are we content to enjoy each other's company and closed to others we might welcome into our group? Are we indifferent to ways we might serve others together? If these elements are present in our community life, what would repentance and faith look like for us as a group?

AN HONEST COMMUNITY

BIG IDEA

Real, authentic community means being known "as we really are." But most of us are worried that others would not accept us or like us if they really knew us. So instead of letting our true selves be known, we hide behind a false self. We put forward a good image. We pretend. This sort of "image management," though it seems innocuous, is actually deeply wicked. It's a subtle form of dishonesty, manipulation, and lying. The apostle John urges us to turn from this darkness, this denial of truth, and "walk in the light" instead. To do that, we need to turn again to what the gospel has to say about who we are. The gospel assures us that God fully approves of us and accepts us in Christ, despite our weaknesses and sins. The more we truly believe this, the more we are freed from slavery to the approval or disapproval of others. We can walk in the light, confident in our identity in Christ, free to be known as we really are and to love others as they really are.

NOTES:

Lesson

ARTICLE

7

AN HONEST COMMUNITY

What is the single most important component of any healthy relationship?

Maybe your initial answer to this question is something like love, trust, or selflessness. But let us suggest an answer that is even deeper and more foundational than any of those: *truth*.

Relationships simply cannot exist without honesty. As soon as I'm dishonest—untruthful—with you, I begin to unravel the sacred bonds of relationship. The starkest examples of this are painfully clear to us: a cheating spouse, an embezzling CEO, a friend who betrays a confidence.

In comparison to these dire examples, we often convince ourselves that we're pretty truthful. But in reality, the fall has made us all liars. We don't want people to know us as we really are. We want to appear a certain way—to be known as a certain kind of person. So we put forth an "image," a public face. Author Brennan Manning refers to this as "the Impostor:"

> The impostor is the classic codependent. To gain acceptance and approval, the false self suppresses or camouflages feelings, making emotional honesty impossible. [We] present a perfect image to the public so that everybody will admire us and nobody will know us. . . . The impostor prompts us to attach importance to what has no importance, clothing with a false glitter what is least substantial and turning us away from what

is real. The false self causes us to live in a world of delusion. The impostor is a liar.*

Christians are skilled at playing the impostor. It's exactly what Adam and Eve did in the garden of Eden. When God created them, they were "naked and were not ashamed" (Genesis 2:25). But once they sinned, they began to hide. They became aware of their nakedness and "sewed fig leaves together" (Genesis 3:7). Rather than being fully transparent, they were ashamed and began to withhold things from each other and from God. And we've been doing the same thing ever since.

This is the reason Christian community is often shallow and stagnant. The apostle John calls it "walking in darkness." And his remedy is *truth*— or, as he puts it, "walking in the light":

> God is light, and in him is no darkness at all. If we say we have fellowship with him while we walk in darkness, we lie and do not practice the truth. But if we walk in the light, as he is in the light, we have fellowship with one another, and the blood of Jesus his Son cleanses us from all sin. If we say we have no sin, we deceive ourselves, and the truth is not in us. If we confess our sins, he is faithful and just to forgive us our sins and to cleanse us from all unrighteousness. (1 John 1:5–9)

If we walk in the light, as God is in the light, we have fellowship with one another. We have true community. We have real relationship. We're finished pretending, hiding, covering up. You know the real me and I know the real you. And that's a good recipe for true friendship.

But *how* can we consistently walk in the light? What gives us the freedom to live in honesty and truth with one another? It's the gospel. It's faith working through love. It's "the blood of Jesus cleansing us from all sin." Only when we've really come to Jesus in repentance and faith will we experience the kind of honest community we long for. Because only in Jesus is our struggle for righteousness and identity resolved.

---

*   Brennan Manning, *Abba's Child* (Colorado Springs, CO: NavPress, 2002), 31.

Pause and ask yourself another question: What's the worst thing someone could possibly know about you?

Now, what if everyone in your church community knew that? What would you stand to lose? What you'd probably lose is (1) their approval and (2) your sense of righteousness. They would know the real truth about you (and perhaps not approve of you)! And you would have to admit the truth about yourself (you couldn't pretend to be "righteous" anymore)! In other words, walking in the light would directly confront your thirst for approval and your unwarranted self-righteousness. The reason you avoid honesty is because you're still striving to maintain your own identity and construct your own righteousness.

Here's another way to say the same thing: Dishonesty is rooted in unbelief. It's a gospel issue. When I'm not resting in the identity and righteousness I have in Christ, I'll be tempted to "save face" or keep up appearances. I'll want to make sure people have a certain impression of me.

But the gospel frees us from this! The good news of the gospel is that your identity is in Christ, not in what people think of you. And your righteousness comes from Christ, not your good behavior (or good reputation). You don't have to keep up appearances. You don't have to manage your image. You don't have to save face. Jesus gives you a new identity and a righteousness you did not possess or earn on your own. They are yours by grace. You can rest in the identity and righteousness that Jesus provides. And so you can freely walk in the light with the people around you. You no longer need to sew together fig leaves; God himself has clothed you in the righteousness of his Son. "I will greatly rejoice in the LORD, my soul shall exult in my God, for he has clothed me with the garments of salvation; he has covered me with the robe of righteousness" (Isaiah 61:10).

A community where the truth of the gospel is deeply believed, reflected on, and talked about will be a community of healthy, transformative honesty. It will be a community where people increasingly find their identity in Christ and not in the approval of others; a community where self-righteousness gives way to faith-righteousness; a community where people are loved as they really are but loved too much to let them stay that way. It will be a community of radical grace, generous hospitality, and joyful humility. It will be a community of light, truth, goodness and beauty, where the glory of God is on display to the world.

Isn't that the kind of community you want? It all starts with you and me walking in the light.

SPEAKING THE TRUTH IN LOVE

There are two aspects to being honest with people: Telling the truth about ourselves and telling the truth about others. Both are necessary if we want true relationship. But we all know that truth-telling, by itself, can be selfish and hurtful. That is why Paul says that "speaking the truth *in love*, we are to grow up in every way . . . " (Ephesians 4:15). To love people is to will their good, so our truth-telling must have that aim. This verse holds together all the tension surrounding the issue of honesty. It doesn't let us sweep things under the rug, but neither does it let us vent our thoughts and feelings on anyone and everyone around us. We must speak the truth and we must do it for the purpose of building others up in love.

This exercise is designed to help us grow in telling the truth about ourselves and others. We want to uncover the unbelief and idolatry underneath our dishonesty, consider how the truths of the gospel apply, and see how looking to Jesus frees us to walk in the light and be honest, both as individuals and as a community.

TELLING THE TRUTH ABOUT OURSELVES

1. Think of something you would not want people to know about you. Just asking the question probably brings something to mind right away. If not, take a minute to ask God to bring something to mind.

We're not going to ask you to tell the group what it is, but the rest of the exercise assumes you have something in mind.

2. **Identify the Idol**: Now ask yourself: Why do you want to keep that hidden? Below are some possible answers to that question. Mark the one that most represents why you would not want to tell people the thing you have in mind:

- If people knew the whole truth about me, they probably wouldn't like me (approval).
- If people knew the whole truth about me, who knows how they'd react? I wouldn't be able to control their opinion of me (control/manipulation).
- If people knew the whole truth about me, I might lose standing or respect in their eyes (respect).
- If people knew the whole truth about me, who knows what they'd do with that information? They could tell others (reputation).

3. **Look to Jesus**: How did Jesus triumph over this idol? How do we see, in his life, death, and resurrection, a refusal to live for these things? And how is what he gives us far better?

4. **Believe the gospel**: What truths about God or about your new identity in Christ aren't you believing? How does resting in the good news of the gospel free you to be honest about yourself?

SPEAKING THE TRUTH TO OTHERS

There are certainly good reasons not to say everything we think about others. However, our failure to speak truth to others often reflects a lack of love. Rather than caring about the other person, we're more worried about how he or she might react.

1. Consider the following hypothetical scenarios:

- In your small group, someone shares a viewpoint that doesn't line up with what is really true or good. Instead of challenging the opinion or engaging the person in further conversation, you (and the rest of the group) "let it go."

- A single woman is asked on a date by a guy she's not really interested in. Instead of just telling him the truth, she finds some other reason to say no.
- Someone in your small group is sarcastic with everyone. His sarcasm keeps him from having any really meaningful conversations, and it often hurts or offends people. Instead of saying something, you (and the rest of the group) avoid confrontation, and the pattern continues.

2. Identify the Idol: In facing these scenarios or others like them, what do you find yourself thinking?

- "They probably have enough to think about. I don't want to add more to their plate" (approval).
- "I'm not sure he can handle the truth. It's probably more loving to be polite or just let it go" (control/manipulation).
- "I don't want to have to explain myself, sort out misunderstandings, or get into a debate" (comfort).
- "I don't want to be the guy who's always creating conflict" (reputation).

3. Look to Jesus: Again, how did Jesus triumph over this idol? How do we see, in his life, death, and resurrection, a refusal to live for these things? And how is what he gives us far better?

4. Believe the gospel: What truths about God or about your new identity in Christ aren't you believing? How does resting in your identity in Christ confront your idolatry and free you to speak the truth in love to others?

An example, using the surface sin of not speaking the truth about ourselves:

(1) Identify the idol (sin beneath the sin)	(2) Look to Jesus	(3) Believe the gospel
I fear that people won't like me. I want their approval more than I want to be honest.	Jesus did not seek the approval of men but rested in the words of his Father: "This is my beloved Son, in whom I am well-pleased."	God knows everything about me and still loves me. I have been justified by faith in Jesus. I can be honest about my sin because I do not need the approval of others to prove myself.
I don't know how people will react to the real me. I want to control/manipulate their view of me more than I want to be honest.	Jesus is the image of the invisible God. In his very existence, he is personal revelation. He did not manipulate or control public opinion. He spoke the truth concerning himself and was, in fact, killed for it.	God is in control. Even if people seek to harm me, God takes what others intend for harm and works it for my good. I am free to be honest about myself and to trust God no matter how people respond.
I want to be respected by others more than I want to be honest with them.	Jesus laid aside his right to be respected, humbling himself to the point of death.	I am not respectable in God's eyes, but God sent Jesus to die for the ungodly. My worth is not based on my performance, but on the fact that I am a son/daughter of God.
I fear that people will tell others about my sin and ruin my reputation. I want to protect my reputation more than I want to be honest.	Jesus was sinless and people still sought to ruin his reputation. He did not defend himself but rather entrusted himself to God. He was more concerned with God's glory than his reputation.	The gospel makes me an ambassador for God and his kingdom. My primary concern, therefore, is his reputation and not mine. When I am mistreated by others, my humility and forgiving spirit put the gospel on display to those around me.

A GRACE-FILLED COMMUNITY

BIG IDEA

Because we are made in the image of God, we all long to be part of an accepting, loving community. But sin has distorted our understanding and tainted our desires in this area. Sometimes we settle for a flimsy sort of "acceptance" that doesn't confront unbiblical beliefs or behaviors. In other situations we can make people earn our acceptance through their performance. Our deep dysfunction in this area is only healed when we allow the gospel to transform our hearts and lives. When we understand and believe that God accepts and forgives us in Christ, we gain a right understanding of what it means to accept and forgive each other. And as we walk in the power of God's Spirit, we live according to a new set of desires and abilities. This is how the gospel forms a grace-filled community.

NOTES:

A GRACE-FILLED COMMUNITY

God's "varied grace" (1 Peter 4:10) is multifaceted in its effects and manifold in its beauty. It saves, blesses, secures, sanctifies, enables, and sustains us. But how does grace shape a community? To answer that question, let's first consider the hindrances to grace in our hearts: **pride** and **fear**.

In our **pride**, we don't just want to be accepted; we want to be *acceptable*. Have you ever told God that you would "never do that again"? If you can just get a fresh start, you will do better? We may think we are asking for grace, but what we really want is a second chance to earn God's favor. But grace is *unmerited*, undeserved favor: "God shows his love for us in that while we were still sinners, Christ died for us" (Romans 5:8). Pride also gets in the way of forgiveness. Do you ever find yourself explaining your sin to God rather than confessing it? Blaming people or circumstances, claiming ignorance, comparing yourself to others? We want to justify ourselves before God, but the Bible says we have been "justified by his grace" (Titus 3:7).

In our **fear**, we are pretty sure that God does not accept us. We don't want to talk to God about our sin because we imagine that he is tired of having the same conversation over and over. Or we think that God cannot forgive what we have done. Rather than ask for forgiveness, we try to hide our sin from God because we fear his rejection. The good news is that Jesus "gave himself for us to redeem us from **all** lawlessness and to purify for himself a people for his own possession" (Titus 2:14).

A gospel-centered community begins with people who are growing in grace. As we receive God's grace toward us in Christ, we are able to give grace to others. We can "welcome one another as Christ has welcomed [us]" (Romans 15:7), and we can "forgiv[e] one other as God in Christ forgave [us]" (Ephesians 4:32). However, if we want to be conduits of grace to one another, we must confront the various ways that pride and fear hinder the flow of grace in our relationships.

Our **pride** manifests itself in a desire to measure up—to do whatever we think will earn people's approval. That varies, of course, depending on what your community values most. In the first century, you were "in" if you were circumcised, kept the dietary laws, and observed the Sabbath. In many churches today, being accepted as an insider means reading the right books, voting for the right political candidate, being passionate or vulnerable, serving the poor, or speaking the right lingo. We earn acceptance by living up to the standards of the community and we offer acceptance on the same basis. Sometimes we withhold forgiveness from those who have hurt us deeply or who don't "deserve" it yet.

Consider a few examples of how pride short-circuits the work of God's grace in community.

- Stacey rarely talks during her small group discussions. When her group leader asked her about it, she shared that she doesn't want to talk unless she knows exactly what she is going to say. She wants to say the right things so that people will accept her. In this case, Stacey's pride (or fear) keeps her from engaging in honest discussion.
- Steve loves his small group. It is the highlight of his week and he is a faithful, prepared participant. Its members are his main social network and he often expresses how much he appreciates being vulnerable and open with people he trusts. But when others are invited to visit the group, Steve is aloof and says little. He explains that he is unwilling to share personal things with people who haven't proven themselves to be trustworthy. He wishes the group could be closed to "outsiders" so that he could be himself. His desire for control leads him to reject anyone new.

Our fear manifests itself in a desire to protect ourselves. We think people would not like us if they really knew us. Consequently, we don't want to ask for forgiveness because that means admitting the full extent of our sin. We don't want to be judged or rejected, so we cover our sin. We excuse it, blame it on others, downplay it, hide it, lie about it, anything but admit it and ask for forgiveness. Think about your relationships: How often do people in your community admit that they have sinned against someone and ask for forgiveness? We usually stop short of this because we are afraid of being known as we really are. Here are a couple of examples.

- When Kyle's wife caught him viewing pornography, he said he was sorry, but he didn't acknowledge the offense against his wife and the consequences of his sin. Instead he tried to explain that his behavior was pretty common for guys and that he didn't do it very often compared to a lot of guys he knows. When his wife asked him to talk to the men in their small group about it and seek their help, Kyle resisted. He said they probably did the same thing, but if they didn't, he did not want them to think of him as perverted or weak. He minimized his sin rather than confessing it.

- Mary was afraid to tell her new community group about her battle with anxiety. She was sure that people would treat her differently if they knew. She managed to keep it hidden for a while, but one night she had a panic attack in the middle of the group discussion. She felt exposed and embarrassed but then something unexpected happened. Nobody freaked out. In fact, they prayed with her, talked her through it, and then went on with the discussion. That night freed Mary from her self-concern and enabled her to focus on the needs of others.

So how does the gospel work to create a grace-filled community? To put it simply, the gospel puts to death the pride and fear that hinder our relationships with God and others.

Let's use 1 Peter 3:18 as a framework to see how this happens: "For Christ also suffered once for sins, the righteous for the unrighteous, that he might bring us to God, being put to death in the flesh but made alive in the Spirit."

Though Jesus was without sin, he suffered the consequences of sin in his community. His own people did not receive him (John 1:11). His closest friends betrayed and denied him (Mark 14:10, 71). He was mocked and murdered by those who did not understand him (Mark 15:16–32). Jesus suffered these things for us, "the righteous for the unrighteous." We are no different from those who rejected and persecuted Jesus. We cultivate anger and contempt in our hearts toward people made in the image of God. We pretend to be something we are not. We go behind people's backs to gossip and steal. We are passive-aggressive. We manipulate people and situations to get our own way. We put others down to feel better about ourselves. This is the bad news: Our own sin is the thing that hinders the flow of grace in our community.

But the good news is that Jesus suffered and died on our behalf, "that he might bring us to God." When we *receive* the grace of God toward us in Christ, our fear and pride are put to death, and we are brought to life spiritually by God's gracious Holy Spirit.

- In our *pride*, we show favoritism toward those we like or who can help us, but Jesus sought out the outcasts and welcomed them in. Now by his Spirit we "show no partiality" (James 2:1).
- In our *pride*, we are envious when good things happen to others, but Jesus placed our good before his own. Now by his Spirit we "rejoice with those who rejoice, [and] weep with those who weep" (Romans 12:15).
- In our *pride,* we harbor offenses and are unwilling to forgive, but Jesus forgave both his enemies who crucified him and his friends who deserted him. Now by his Spirit we "bear with one another . . . and forgive each other" (Colossians 3:13).
- In our *fear*, we exert our power to control people and situations, but Jesus restrained his power and went willingly to the cross. Now by his Spirit we can walk in "humility and gentleness" (Ephesians 4:2).

- In our *fear*, we want to run when relationships get difficult, but Jesus endured the cross for those who sinned against him. Now by his Spirit we "bear with one another in love" (Ephesians 4:2).
- In our *fear,* we are afraid to confront the sins of others, but Jesus dealt honestly with sin wherever he encountered it. Now by his Spirit we can gently restore those who are caught in a transgression (Galatians 6:1).

Becoming a grace-filled community requires us to identify our tendencies toward pride and fear, look to Jesus to be freed from our pride and fear, and then freely love others as God has loved us, in dependence on the Holy Spirit. This week's exercise will help us with all three things.

Lesson

EXERCISE

GROWING IN GRACE

One of the greatest blessings of the gospel is the presence and power of the Holy Spirit, who lives within every one of God's people (Romans 8:9–11). To grow in grace means to continually rely on the Spirit's power rather than on our own instincts or preferences.

The chart on the next page identifies six specific ways that our pride and fear hinder community. Identify which tendencies are present in your life and then consider how the Holy Spirit frees and empowers you to live differently. Spend some time in prayer repenting of sin and asking the Spirit to reign in your community.

SIX SPECIFIC WAYS THAT OUR PRIDE AND FEAR HINDER COMMUNITY:

These Sinful (Non-Accepting) Tendencies	Are Rooted in Pride or Fear	Here's How Gospel-Driven, Spirit-Led Acceptance Would Look Different
Favoritism: I show preference toward those I like or those who can help me.	These people have earned my respect. They have something I need. They are more desirable than others who have less to offer.	"Show no partiality" (James 2:1). The Spirit empowers me to treat every person with love, patience, and kindness, honoring them as image bearers of God.
Control: I exert my power to control or manipulate people or situations.	I am trying to manipulate these people to do what is "right" in my eyes. If they do what I want, I am more accepting of them.	"Humility and gentleness" (Ephesians 4:2). The Spirit moves me to humility (my rules are not the standard), which frees me to love others whether or not they "play by my rules."
Avoidance: I flee or avoid when relationships get difficult.	These people are not living up to what I expect of them, so they're not worthy of my acceptance. I guess that's "just the way these people are" (but if they want to be that way, I don't want to relate to them).	"Bear with one another in love" (Ephesians 4:2). The Spirit gives me patience to bear with others, love to believe the best about them, and faithfulness to stay engaged with them despite their faults and failures. I am empowered to move toward them as God moved toward me.
Peacekeeping: I am hesitant to confront the sins of others	Everyone has faults and weaknesses. Who am I to confront someone else?	"Restore others in a spirit of gentleness" (Galatians 6:1). The Spirit gives me a true love for others that yearns to see them glorify God fully. I am grieved by their sin (not just annoyed with it) and motivated by love to confront them in a spirit of gentleness.
Party Spirit: I just relate better to "these people" rather than "those people."	"These people" are more like me (therefore I uncritically accept whatever they believe, say, or do). After all, what they believe, say, or do is right!	"May there be no divisions among you" (1 Corinthians 1:10). The Spirit brings unity and peace within the whole body of Christ, causing me to love those unlike me. The Spirit triumphs over classism, racism, cliques, factions, and divisions.
Unforgiving Spirit: I just can't forgive this person or these people; their offenses against me are too willful, too consistent, or too hurtful.	I'm not as bad/hurtful as they are; their sin against me is much worse than my sin against God and others. If I forgave them, they'd essentially "get away with it." Justice wouldn't be served.	"Bearing with one another and, if one has a complaint against another, forgiving each other" (Colossians 3:13). The Spirit empowers me to be gracious and forgiving toward the faults and failures of others. I can trust God to bring redemption and justice.

Lesson

9

A MISSIONAL COMMUNITY

BIG IDEA

Since Lesson 5, we have been exploring some of the defining marks of a biblical community: joy, humility, honesty, and grace. In this last lesson, we're going to consider one final characteristic of a gospel-centered community: mission. A gospel-centered community is a community that is *moving toward others as God has moved toward them*. Moving toward others is what traditional missionaries do when they leave their homeland and go to a foreign culture. Although everyone isn't called to move far from home to share the gospel, all Christians are called to leave their comfortable routines and move toward their neighbors who don't know Christ. The Father sent the Son; the Son sent the Spirit; and the Spirit sends the church. As those changed by the Spirit through the gospel, we are a "going" people, always moving toward others as God has moved toward us.

NOTES:

A MISSIONAL COMMUNITY

Now that we've reached the last lesson of this study, let's review where we've been. We began in Lesson 1 with a biblical theology of community: God made us for community; sin destroys community; Jesus redeems us *for* community and *in* community. In Lessons 2 and 3, we considered how community shapes our understanding of what Christ has done for us along with our progress in applying it to our lives. We also considered how the gospel works to form and transform our experience of community. In Lesson 4, through the biblical principle of "faith working through love," we saw that our failure to love others is really a failure to believe and apply the truths and promises of the gospel. And in Lessons 5 through 8, we explored some defining marks of a biblical community: joy, humility, honesty, and grace.

We're ready now to consider one final characteristic of a gospel-centered community: *mission*. A gospel-centered community is a *missional* community. If you are a Christian, then you are a sent one, a missionary—you are on mission. Mission isn't just something we do; it's an expression of who we are in Christ. It's a natural overflow of the gospel's renewing work in us.

To set the stage for our conversation, let's consider three common misconceptions about mission and missionaries.

1. The word *missionary* refers only to those who are specially called by God to go to other cultures to preach the gospel.

2. To reach non-Christians with the gospel message, we need to "do things differently"; we need special programs, targeted evangelistic activities, investigative Bible studies, etc.

3. Some people are gifted by God as evangelists to win people to Christ; others are gifted to serve the church and build young Christians into mature disciples.

It's not that these statements are entirely false. The problem is that they shortchange the Bible's teaching about the scope and means of God's mission as explained below. Consider how the verses below extend our understanding:

1. All Christians are missionaries. Being part of God's family means we are all sent to others with the good news of salvation from sin and death. That is part of our identity as the new family of God. Some of us are called to share the gospel with our neighbors across the street. Some of us are called to share the gospel with our neighbors from other countries and cultures. But all Christians are sent by Jesus to bring their faith to the broken world. "As the Father has sent me, even so I am sending you" (John 20:21). "God . . . through Christ reconciled us to himself and gave us the ministry of reconciliation. . . . Therefore, we are ambassadors for Christ, God making his appeal through us" (2 Corinthians 5:18–20).

2. There is a time and place for special events and strategies. However, Scripture and history make clear that God intends to reach non-Christians through the normal activity of the church. Paul assumes that unbelievers will be present in church gatherings: "If all prophesy, and an unbeliever or outsider enters, he is convicted by all, he is called to account by all, the secrets of his heart are disclosed, and so, falling on his face, he will worship God and declare that God is really among you" (1 Corinthians 14:24–25). And the church in Acts saw many people saved through the normal rhythms of worship and community: "And day by day, attending the temple together and breaking bread in their homes, they received their food with glad and generous hearts, praising God and having favor with all the people. And the Lord added to their number day by day those who were being saved" (Acts 2:46–47). When the church was scattered in Acts 8, "those

who were scattered went about preaching the word [of God]" (Acts 8:4). The mission of God goes forward through the people of God, wherever they are and in whatever they do.

3. No gift or personality type is exempt from the mission of God through the church. There is diversity in our gifts and roles, but unity in our calling. Every Christian is called to Christ's mission: "Go therefore and make disciples of all nations, baptizing them in the name of the Father and of the Son and of the Holy Spirit [evangelism/conversion], teaching them to observe all that I have commanded you [discipleship]" (Matthew 28:19–20). And because the gospel is the key to both conversion and sanctification, evangelism and discipleship are not two different things, but one continuous activity. The mission is to enjoy God and live for his glory—and to help others do the same (1 Corinthians 10:31).

So what does it mean to be a missional community? There are hundreds of ways to answer that question, but for the sake of simplicity, let's focus on one simple idea: *Mission means moving toward others as God has moved toward us.*

Mission means *moving toward.* In Western culture, many churches and Christians have adopted a "come to us" mentality: "We're here and available; if people want to know about Christ, we welcome them." Though this approach is common, it doesn't accurately reflect how God has treated us. If God had waited for us to come to him, we'd still be dead in our sins! Before God saved us, we were "foolish, disobedient, deceived and enslaved by all kinds of passions and pleasures" (Titus 3:3 NIV). We weren't seeking God, so God deliberately moved toward us. He stepped out of heaven and into time and space and history: "The Word became flesh and dwelt among us" (John 1:14). The message of the gospel is that God moves toward us while we are running in the opposite direction. So, as we follow Jesus into mission, we don't merely wait for others to come to us. We take the initiative. We go to them.

Mission is concerned for *others.* Throughout the Bible we see God's persistent concern for the stranger, the outsider, and the sojourner.

He instructed Moses: "You shall treat the stranger who sojourns with you as the native among you, and you shall love him as yourself, for you were strangers in the land of Egypt: I am the LORD your God" (Leviticus 19:34). And he encouraged Paul in the pagan city of Corinth: "Go on speaking and do not be silent; for I am with you . . . I have many people in this city" (Acts 18:9–10 NASB). Like our Father in heaven, we long to see strangers become friends. We long to see those who are alienated from God reconciled to him. So we do *everything* in a way that's hospitable toward unbelievers. In our prayer meetings, our worship services, and our community groups, we *expect* non-Christians to be present. We are always thinking about how to welcome them, how to serve them, and how to love them.

Mission is rooted in the way *God has moved toward us*. A missional posture can be sustained by sheer will power . . . for awhile. But not for the long haul. Consistently moving toward others as God has moved toward us will bring us into constant conflict with the idols of comfort, control, and approval. The only thing that can defeat these idols and empower us to live a life of mission is a constant remembering and rejoicing in what Jesus has done for us.

A gospel-centered community is a community of people who are increasingly orienting their lives around God's mission. They are moving toward others as God has moved toward them. They are looking for opportunities to bless and serve others so that more and more people might become worshipers of Jesus. They are talking about both the heart foundation of mission (their joy, love, delight in Jesus) and the practical implications of mission (how they will live on mission together). They are becoming disciples who make more disciples.

We want you to spend the rest of this lesson talking honestly about how *your* community is doing in mission. The exercise at the end of the lesson gives a number of helpful questions through which you can assess your life together. Indulge in a free-flowing, honest, gracious conversation, and may you experience God's Spirit moving toward you so that you might move toward others.

LIVING ON MISSION

This week's exercise is designed to stir up some good, healthy, formative conversation about how you are doing as a *missional* community. How you answer these questions will depend somewhat on the kind of group you are: the questions can apply to a whole church, a community group, a mission team, or a dozen other possibilities. Maybe you'll get to all the questions or maybe you'll only focus on a few. Either way, be gracious and truthful as you offer your reflections, and listen carefully to the thoughts of others. Rest assured, the Holy Spirit wants to move God's people out into mission. Satan wants to keep that from happening.

Mission means moving toward others
as God has moved toward us.

IN RELATIONSHIP

- Does each person in our group have genuine friendships with non-Christians? (The mark of this is not whether *you* would call particular non-Christians your friends, but whether *they* would call *you* their friend.)
- Does our group create space to engage those relationships together? Are we a group of isolated Christians living individual lives or are we living on mission together? Do we know each other's non-Christian friends?

REPENT: What sin do we need to repent of?
BELIEVE: What grace do we need to ask for and expect?

ACT: What practical action do we need to take? Who will take the lead?

IN PRAYER

- Are we praying *together* for specific non-Christians in our lives and neighborhoods?
- Do we pray big, kingdom-oriented prayers—for conversion of unbelievers, for conviction of sin, for God's kingdom to come and his will to be done in our city, for the nations? Or do our prayers tend to be focused on our own needs and problems?
- Would our prayers give the impression, to an outsider, that we actually *believe* in a sovereign, gracious, glorious, beautiful, holy God?

REPENT: What sin do we need to repent of?
BELIEVE: What grace do we need to ask for and expect?
ACT: What practical action do we need to take? Who will take the lead?

IN LANGUAGE AND POSTURE

- Is our language accessible to outsiders? Or do our conversations tend to be sprinkled with Christian lingo, inside jokes, or church references that only make sense to our "tribe"?
- Do we speak positively of our city and of those who don't know Christ? Do we have appropriate gospel humility—not taking ourselves too seriously, admitting our weaknesses, not being defensive or rude toward our critics? Are unbelievers glad to know us, even if they don't believe the gospel?
- Do we talk about the need for gospel work around the world, giving a voice in our community to those who may otherwise go unnoticed?

REPENT: What sin do we need to repent of?
BELIEVE: What grace do we need to ask for and expect?

ACT: What practical action do we need to take? Who will take the lead?

IN ACTIVITY AND PRESENCE

- Do we gather in a place that non-Christians find hospitable and welcoming? Is there anything about our place of meeting, our time of meeting, or the dynamics of our gathering that would make it difficult for an outsider to enter in?
- Are we actively engaging the neighborhood in which we gather? Or do we drop in, study the Bible, and head out again? Do non-Christians see us working for the good of the neighborhood or only furthering the needs of our own group?
- How are we involved in the mission of God to other places and cultures—either sending or going?

REPENT: What sin do we need to repent of?
BELIEVE: What grace do we need to ask for and expect?
ACT: What practical action do we need to take? Who will take the lead?

Close with a time of prayer, repenting of sin and asking God for the grace you need to be faithful to the missional calling he has given you as individuals and a group. Thank him for his promise to give you what you need to move toward others as he has moved toward you.

LEADER'S GUIDE

The Gospel-Centered Community is designed for small group study. The tone of the material assumes a small-group format because this is the setting we've found to be the most effective.

Each lesson is designed to take around seventy-five minutes to complete. If your group has more time available, you can simply spend a little longer in the Discussion and Exercise sections. Our experience has shown that this content often creates deep and substantive conversation that can easily last longer than seventy-five minutes. So plan accordingly, and be sure to honor the time commitment that your group has made.

Because *The Gospel-Centered Community* is designed as an introduction to the dynamics of gospel renewal and its impact on community life, there is no outside work required of participants. Each person should simply receive a copy of the study guide. The content will often stimulate further reflection over the following days, but no preparation is needed for subsequent lessons.

Likewise, it is not assumed that the group leader will be an expert theologian or longstanding Christian. Ample direction and content is provided in this leader's guide to help the leader facilitate the group's time together. The material also provides the content for the study, so there is no need for the group leader to try and "teach" the group. Just relax and guide a good conversation.

Lesson

LEADER'S GUIDE

CREATED FOR COMMUNITY

FORMAT OVERVIEW

I. BIBLE CONVERSATION // Read and talk about the passage(s)

II. ARTICLE // Read "Created for Community" together

III. DISCUSSION // Process concepts together

IV. EXERCISE // Apply the concepts using the "Five Indicators of Individualism" exercise

V. WRAP-UP // Final thoughts and prayer

BIBLE CONVERSATION *(10 minutes)*

The purpose of this Bible conversation is to lay the biblical foundation for community, which is the fact that we are made in the image of a Trinitarian, relational God. Your goal is simply to get the discussion going in a way that establishes a biblical foundation for the concepts that will be explored throughout the study. So don't aim for deep Hebrew exegesis. Instead, aim to make some basic observations about the passage.

SET-UP (BROAD) Tonight we're launching into some new content that's intended to help us think about how the gospel affects community. Each week, we'll talk about a Bible passage, read a short article, discuss some concepts, and do an exercise to help us apply what we learn. Content like this can either be stiff and dry or rich and formative, depending on how we engage it. So let's commit together to give careful thought to what we read *and* draw each other out as we talk.

SET-UP (LESSON 1) Among world religions, there are basically two views of God: monotheism (one God) and polytheism (many gods). But among the great monotheistic religions—Judaism, Islam, and Christianity—the Christian view of God is distinct. Christians believe that God is a Trinity or a Tri-unity: one being in three persons. As we start our discussion, we want to look at a Bible passage that lays the foundation for this doctrine. The passage is Genesis 1:26–27.

READ *Have someone read Genesis 1:26–27 aloud.*

ASK What are some things we learn about God in this passage?

What are some things we learn about humanity in this passage?

If humans are made in the image of a Trinitarian God, what are some of the implications of that?

TRANSITION TO ARTICLE One of the implications of being made in God's image is that we have a deep longing for community. Let's read this article, "Created for Community," together to process that reality more deeply.

ARTICLE *(10 minutes)*

The point of reading an article together is twofold: (1) To explain key concepts so that everyone in your group has a common understanding and vocabulary and (2) to provide a focus for conversation. We want to help your group learn how to talk about the gospel in relation to their actual lives. In many cases, people do not talk about what Jesus did for them or what this means for their lives because they simply don't have much to say. The article gives them content to talk about.

READ THE ARTICLE TOGETHER *Read "Created for Community" aloud together, taking turns at paragraph breaks.*

TRANSITION TO DISCUSSION Let's talk about this article for a few minutes. As we do, I'll ask some questions to help us apply these concepts to our daily lives. If there is something you don't "get," by all means ask questions so we can talk it through together.

DISCUSSION *(15–20 minutes)*

1. Which statement or insight in this article stood out to you the most?

2. Genesis 1 helps us see why we all desire meaningful relationships (we were made for them). Let's talk about that at a deeper level.
   o In what ways do you feel like you are experiencing meaningful community?
   o What desires for community (or aspects of community) do you feel are lacking in your life?

3. In the section "The Fall: Broken Community," the article says, "There's something selfish and self-absorbed about us that [hinders community]." How do you see this in your own life?

4. The article concludes by talking about community as the context for transformation. How do you feel about being part of a community that knows your flaws and failures? What's exciting about that, and what's scary about that?

5. Taking it one step further, what do you think keeps a *community* from becoming selfish and self-absorbed?

TRANSITION TO EXERCISE Building a gospel-centered community is going to require each of us to be honest about how our selfishness specifically affects our relationships. Let's do an exercise that will help us dig a little deeper. *(Turn to the "Five Indicators of Individualism" exercise.)*

EXERCISE *(15–20 minutes)*

SET-UP *Read the introductory paragraph to the exercise.* Let's take a few minutes to read these. Try to pick one or two you most identify with, and then we'll discuss it as a group.

1. Which bullet-point expressions of individualism do you most identify with?

2. How do your particular expressions of individualism reveal selfishness? Be specific: How do they fundamentally make life about *you*?

3. Let's talk about the question at the end: "If your self-centeredness were turned into a joyful God-centeredness, what would be the results for yourself and for the community around you?"

TRANSITION TO WRAP-UP This has been really good. Thanks for sharing. We are going to continue working through these concepts over the next two weeks. Before we wrap up, does anyone have any lingering questions or comments? Okay, let's spend a few minutes praying together. If some of you want to pray, I will close us in a few minutes.

WRAP-UP

Questions, Comments, Prayer

LEADER'S
GUIDE

HOW COMMUNITY SHAPES US IN THE GOSPEL

FORMAT OVERVIEW

I.   BIBLE CONVERSATION // Read and talk about the passage(s)

II. ARTICLE // Read "How Community Shapes Us in the Gospel" together

III. DISCUSSION // Process concepts together

IV. EXERCISE // Work through the "Redemption in Community" exercise together

V.   WRAP-UP // Final thoughts and prayer

BIBLE CONVERSATION *(10 minutes)*

Remember, the goal of the Bible conversation is simply to get the dialogue started. You don't need to exhaustively study the passage; you just need to get people thinking and talking about Scripture. The article will flesh out the implications of the passage in greater detail.

SET-UP To start our discussion tonight, we're going to read a passage of Scripture and talk about it for a few minutes. The goal isn't to exhaustively study the passage, but just to consider it and let it sink in. So let's read it and then I'll ask a couple of questions to spur some discussion.

READ *Have someone read Romans 11:33–36 aloud.*

ASK What truths about God are highlighted in this passage? Let's list as many as we can. *(God's wisdom and knowledge are rich and deep; his ways are beyond us; no one has given him anything; he doesn't "owe us" anything; all things are from him (Creator) and through him (Sustainer) and for him (Purpose/Goal/End, etc.).*

What sorts of feelings or responses does this passage stir up within you? Why? *(The passage is clearly doxological, which means that its intent is to inspire worship. Hopefully that will be true for some of your group members. Other things it might evoke include questions, perplexity, humility, thankfulness, confusion, and perhaps even anger or frustration.)*

TRANSITION TO ARTICLE If "all things" are really from God and for God, then that includes **community.** This article, "How Community Shapes Us in the Gospel," will help us think about how community is actually about God and not about us. Let's read it together.

ARTICLE *(10 minutes)*

READ THE ARTICLE TOGETHER *Read "How Community Shapes Us in the Gospel" aloud together, taking turns at paragraph breaks.*

TRANSITION TO DISCUSSION Let's talk about this article for a few minutes, and then we'll move to the exercise.

DISCUSSION *(10 minutes)*

1. What stood out to you in the article? What are your initial thoughts/reactions?

2. Look at the bullet points that contrast "me at the center" and "God at the center." Which of them resonates most with you?

Which have you seen in your experience? *(Go around the room to allow everyone to answer.)*

EXERCISE *(30–45 minutes)*

SET-UP *Read aloud the introductory paragraph of the "Redemption in Community" exercise. Give people a few minutes to think through the questions, and then invite them to discuss their answers with one another.*

Because of the example in the article, this week's exercise should be fairly easy for people to grasp. Don't be afraid to call on people directly in order to spur discussion. It's okay if you don't get to everyone in the group; the coming weeks will provide plenty of opportunity for conversation.

As leader, focus on helping your group answer questions 3 and 4. Identifying a situation (question 1) should be the easy part. Identifying the heart response (question 2) may be a little more challenging for some people (and you can certainly invite the rest of the group to help). But questions 3 and 4 get down to the nitty-gritty of gospel application. If you get stuck or need some help, look back to the article and the example given there.

CLOSE Thanks, [name] and [name], for sharing with the rest of us. We'll continue to talk about these themes in coming weeks. For now, let's close in prayer, asking God to use us to spur spiritual formation in each other. Let's ask God to make us a *formative* community, not just a *functional* one.

WRAP-UP

Questions, Comments, Prayer

HOW THE GOSPEL SHAPES COMMUNITY

FORMAT OVERVIEW

I.   BIBLE CONVERSATION // Read and talk about the passage(s)

II. ARTICLE // Read "Community Barriers and Gospel Freedom" together

III. DISCUSSION // Process concepts together

IV. EXERCISE // [contained within article]

V.   COMMUNAL WORSHIP AND PRAYER // Special closing exercise

BIBLE CONVERSATION *(10 minutes)*

In this lesson, we're going to read a very short passage. Don't let this part of the conversation take very long—the answers aren't rocket science. The goal is to reflect on the simple parable Jesus told and to consider what it's teaching us about the kingdom of God.

SET-UP To start our discussion tonight, we're going to read a short teaching from Jesus.

READ *Have someone read Luke 6:32–36 aloud.*

`ASK` What point is Jesus making about human nature? (*It's natural to be good to people who are good to you. It's human nature to like people who like us.*)

Let's apply Jesus' insight to community. How should Christian community be distinct or different from "normal" human community? (*Christian community is counter-intuitive. It should go beyond what's normal. It should be unusual, provocative, and unexplainable—like God's mercy to us.*)

`TRANSITION TO ARTICLE` Christian community is supposed to be unique because of the presence of the Holy Spirit and the power of the gospel among us. This week's article is going to talk more about that.

ARTICLE (*10 minutes*)

`READ THE ARTICLE TOGETHER` *Read "Community Barriers and Gospel Freedom" aloud as a group, taking turns at paragraph breaks.*

`TRANSITION` For the rest of our time, I want us to discuss this article together and interact with one another's answers to the questions it raised. Before we do that, are there any questions about the content of the article itself? Anything unclear or confusing?

DISCUSSION AND EXERCISE (*30-40 minutes*)

1. Let's talk about the barriers to community that we face. What barriers did you identify on the first page of the article? (*Have everyone share.*)

2. Now let's ask the question, "What's underneath that?" Remember, we're not trying to dredge up something that's *not* there; we're trying to uncover what *is* there. So let's serve each other by asking good questions and trying to be honest about what's in our hearts.

Choose someone in the group—perhaps someone you've talked to beforehand or someone you know won't mind sharing—and ask him to answer the question, "What's underneath that?" Walk the person through the "False Beliefs" and "False Sources of Hope" sections. Ask questions like, "Do you see some false beliefs about God, self, or others underneath that barrier? What are those false beliefs?"

If people are unwilling to share or just can't identify any false beliefs, don't push them. However, if they're open to dialogue, ask the rest of the group to chime in. You have to know them well enough to accurately gauge their openness to such input. "What do you guys think might lie underneath Dave's objection? Can you share anything from your own life that might shed light on this? Do you have any questions that might help him process what's in his heart?" Emphasize the goal of being helpful, not critical.

COMMUNAL WORSHIP AND PRAYER

(10–15 minutes)

To close this week's group, we'd like you to practice communal worship and prayer. The goal is to help your group start experiencing gospel community instead of just talking about it.

Read through the Exercise page titled "Communal Prayer and Worship." Then guide your group into worshipful prayer. To honor the group's time and set their expectations, task someone with wrapping up the exercise: "John, would you mind closing us in prayer after about fifteen minutes?"

Lesson

LEADER'S GUIDE

FAITH WORKING THROUGH LOVE

FORMAT OVERVIEW

I.   BIBLE CONVERSATION // Read and talk about the passage(s)

II. ARTICLE // Read "Making It Count" together

III. DISCUSSION // Process concepts together

IV. EXERCISE // Apply the concepts using the exercise, "Faith Working Through Love"

V.   WRAP-UP // Final thoughts and prayer

BIBLE CONVERSATION *(10 minutes)*

The Bible discussion is meant to get things started. Your aim is for people to share their observations about the text and their initial reactions to the discussion questions. You want to cultivate a little tension so that there is a felt need to continue the discussion with the article and exercise.

SET-UP There are a number of places in the Bible where we get a picture of community. One of the most famous passages is in Acts 2. We are going to read and discuss that passage as a way to kick off our discussion.

READ *Have someone read Acts 2:42–45 aloud.*

ASK *What is attractive to you about this community?*

ASK What do you think keeps us from experiencing this kind of community?

TRANSITION TO ARTICLE The article in this lesson speaks to this issue (the things that keep us from this kind of community). Let's read it together.

ARTICLE *(10 minutes)*

READ THE ARTICLE TOGETHER *Read "Making It Count" aloud as a group, taking turns at paragraph breaks.*

TRANSITION TO DISCUSSION Let's talk about this article for a few minutes.

DISCUSSION *(10–15 minutes)*

ASK What stood out to you in the article? Anything particularly interesting or challenging?

ASK The article pointed out that when we're confronted with a command from Scripture, we tend to respond with either **resolution** or **resignation**. Which of those do you see more often in your life? Can you give a recent example?

TRANSITION TO EXERCISE Let's flesh this out even more by working through an exercise together.

EXERCISE *(25–30 minutes)*

SET-UP *This week's exercise, "Faith Working Through Love," is very practical and should promote good conversation. Don't be afraid to call on individuals directly to spur discussion. Questions 1 and 2 should be fairly easy for people to self-identify, but Question 3 may often* require input from others. Encourage the group to speak into each other's lives as needed. If your group does not typically relate to each other this directly, remind them to humbly "speak the truth in love" (Ephesians 4:15) as a way to help other members grow in their confidence in the gospel. **Note:** The sample responses from Dave and Jan in the exercise can help guide these interactions.

For instance, let's say that Shannon, a group member, identifies that she has a hard time being "quick to hear and slow to speak" (Question 1) and identifies a tendency toward resignation in this area (Question 2). However, she can't identify her unbelief (Question 3). Invite the rest of the group to help Shannon consider possible answers to that question.

"Have any of you observed Shannon talking a lot but not listening very well? Do you have any ideas about the form of unbelief that might lie beneath that tendency? Can you think of truths Shannon might be missing about God, herself, and others?"

The group may identify a number of possible scenarios, perhaps based on their own experiences, which may include the following.

- **Pride**: Shannon may have a high view of her thoughts and opinions, thinking that her words carry great weight. (This could reveal unbelief about her own sinfulness or a lack of trust in God's ability to speak through others.)
- **Control**: Shannon may fear that if she doesn't offer her thoughts, the discussion will stall out. (This could reveal a lack of trust in God's sovereignty, the Holy Spirit's power to convict, etc.)
- **Fear/Uncertainty**: Shannon may talk a lot to mask her insecurities about herself. (This would reveal a lack of trust in God's acceptance of her in Christ.)
- **Other Possible Reasons**.

It's important that the group not TELL Shannon which of these is true of her but rather seek to serve her in humility and prayer. In some cases her area of unbelief may be strongly evident; that is, the Spirit may use the things group members share to reveal to Shannon a clear area of her unbelief. In other cases, things won't be as clear

*and the group's role will be to humbly offer wisdom and counsel and
then pray with Shannon for the Holy Spirit to bring clarity and light.*

WRAP-UP

Questions, Comments, Prayer

Lesson

LEADER'S GUIDE

A JOYFUL COMMUNITY

FORMAT OVERVIEW

I.   BIBLE CONVERSATION // Read and talk about the passage(s)

II. ARTICLE // Read "A Joyful Community" together

III. DISCUSSION // Process concepts together

IV. EXERCISE // Apply the concepts using the "Growing in Joy" exercise

V.   WRAP-UP // Final thoughts and prayer

BIBLE CONVERSATION *(10 minutes)*

The Bible discussion is meant to get things started. Your aim is for people to simply share their observations about the text and their initial reactions to the discussion questions. You want to cultivate a little tension so that there is a felt need to explore the issues further in the article and exercise.

SET-UP To get the conversation going, we're going to read just one verse in the New Testament, a short parable Jesus told. As we read it, I want you to focus on the concept of joy in this verse.

READ *Have someone read Matthew 13:44 aloud.*

ASK What causes the man in the parable to have joy?

ASK What does he do because of his joy?

ASK How would you describe joy? How is it similar to or different from happiness or satisfaction?

TRANSITION TO ARTICLE This week's article is going to help us think more deeply about joy.

ARTICLE *(10 minutes)*

READ THE ARTICLE TOGETHER *Read "A Joyful Community" aloud together, taking turns at paragraph breaks.*

TRANSITION TO DISCUSSION Let's talk about this article for a few minutes.

DISCUSSION *(10–15 minutes)*

ASK What stood out to you in the article? Anything particularly interesting or challenging?

ASK The article talked about the difference between *justification* and *sanctification*. Does everyone understand the difference? Any need for clarification? [**Note:** *Here, we're trying to make sure everyone understands the basic ideas. Obviously, these are rich theological truths and we could say much more about them, but this isn't a theology lecture. If there is a need for clarification, you can do one of three things: (1) clarify; (2) ask a theologically astute group member to clarify; (3) assign someone to do some research and come back next week to clarify these concepts more fully to the group.*]

ASK The article warns that we often tend to "base our justification on our sanctification," which leads to despair and discouragement. Do any of you see that tendency in yourselves? What effect does it have on your spiritual life?

TRANSITION TO EXERCISE We want to explore this more fully by working through the exercise "Growing in Joy" together.

EXERCISE *(20–25 minutes)*

This week's exercise is challenging for one simple reason: the goal is to go beyond talking about joy to actually helping people begin to experience joy. That depends a lot on your leadership and on the environment you cultivate within your group. Are your group members detached, cerebral, and shallow in their apprehension of these truths? Or are their hearts warmed, their minds stretched, and their souls encouraged? It's not just knowing the truths of justification by faith that makes them powerful—it's believing them. So, as you prepare for the discussion, make sure to do three things:

- *PRAY.* Ask the Holy Spirit to show up and make the truth real to your group.
- *PREPARE.* Prayerfully, slowly read through Romans 4 and 5 to take in all their rich teaching about justification by faith. Be ready to contribute some answers.
- *LEAD.* Don't be satisfied with detached, cerebral discussion. Be awed by the majesty of justification by faith, and allow your awe and worship to spill over to the rest of your group.

Read the introductory paragraphs to the exercise and lead your group through it. It's self-explanatory.

Note: *It's okay if not everyone shares this week. If the Holy Spirit works deeply in one or two people during this time and the others see and experience how to apply the gospel to those people, it "trains" the whole group in how to believe and experience the gospel more deeply for themselves.*

A HUMBLE COMMUNITY

FORMAT OVERVIEW

I. BIBLE CONVERSATION // Read and talk about the passage(s)

II. ARTICLE // Read "A Humble Community" together

III. DISCUSSION // Process concepts together

IV. EXERCISE // Apply the concepts using the "Pride and Prejudice" exercise

V. WRAP-UP // Final thoughts and prayer

BIBLE CONVERSATION *(10 minutes)*

SET-UP We are going to read a conversation between Jesus and two of his disciples about true greatness. The text is Mark 10:35–45. As we read, pay attention to the different characters in the story and what we can learn from each one.

READ *Ask someone to read Mark 10:35–45 aloud.*

ASK In plain terms, what is it that James and John are after? *Their request is basically a request to be vice-president or cabinet members in Jesus' kingdom. They thought that if they could get into the right positions, they would be able to serve the Messiah—and themselves.*

ASK Why do the other disciples respond the way they do? *Perhaps because they want the same thing James and John do. It's probably not because they understand Jesus any better.*

ASK What point is Jesus trying to make about the kingdom of God? *True greatness is found in serving others, which requires humility. Pride is the enemy of kingdom living.*

TRANSITION TO ARTICLE This interaction with Jesus shows us that the key to true greatness is humble service. So how does that play out in community? Let's read this article to see.

ARTICLE *(10 minutes)*

This week's article aims to show the connection between servant-hood and humility. We cannot just make ourselves humble; rather, we become humble as we follow the example of Jesus and personally experience God's grace to us in Christ. That enables us to form communities that seek to serve not just those within the group, but those who don't know Christ.

READ THE ARTICLE TOGETHER *Read "A Humble Community" aloud, taking turns at paragraph breaks.*

TRANSITION TO DISCUSSION Let's talk about this article for a few minutes.

DISCUSSION *(15-20 minutes)*

These questions aim to help everyone understand the concepts in the article and connect them to their own beliefs and actions.

1. What idea or concept stood out to you most in this article?

2. Look at the chart in the article.

- On the consumer side, which aspects do you identify with personally? How do these tendencies reveal self-concern (pride)? How have you seen this negatively affect your involvement in community?
- On the servant side, which aspects do you identify with personally (either something that you are growing in or an area where you particularly want to grow)? Would you say that you see or experience this kind of humility and servanthood in your community? How do these expressions of love reflect humility?
- The article describes receiving grace as "allow[ing] Jesus to serve us . . . instead of insisting on repaying him." For many people, serving God is really a way to pay him back. How do you see that dynamic in your individual life or in our life together as a group? Are there ways in which we need to repent as individuals or as a group? How would a grace-driven motivation look different?

TRANSITION TO EXERCISE Talking about pride in the abstract is easy; identifying our own tendencies toward pride is harder. The "Pride and Prejudice" exercise is designed to help us see what pride looks like in our hearts.

EXERCISE (15–20 minutes)

The point of this exercise is to help your group identify the particular expressions of pride in their lives. Everyone should be able to identify with some aspect of pride on this list.

SET-UP *Read the introductory paragraph to the exercise.* So let's take a few minutes to do the first part of this exercise. Pick the two or three bullet points you most identify with, and then we'll discuss it together as a group. (*Give two to three minutes for everyone to identify their prideful tendencies.*)

`SAY` Alright. We won't have time for everyone to talk through this exercise, so I'd like to ask two of you to serve as case studies and allow us to talk through the rest of the exercise using your bullet points. (*Either choose two people in advance or ask for two volunteers.*)

Work through the rest of the exercise as a group, using the two volunteers' answers.

`ASK` Now that we've done this on the individual level, do you see ways in which our group as a whole tends to be more consumer-oriented than servant-oriented? What might our group look like in our priorities and actions if we were more intentional about being humble servants—to each other and to people outside the group?

`TRANSITION TO WRAP-UP` Thanks, especially [Volunteers A and B], for sharing. Now let's spend a few minutes asking God to deal with the pride in our hearts and help us become more like Jesus as individuals and as a group. If some of you want to pray, I will close us in a few minutes.

WRAP-UP

Questions, Comments, Prayer

AN HONEST COMMUNITY

FORMAT OVERVIEW

I. BIBLE CONVERSATION // Read and talk about the passage(s)

II. ARTICLE // Read "An Honest Community" together

III. DISCUSSION // Process concepts together

IV. FXERCISE // Apply the concepts using the "Speaking the Truth in Love" exercise

V. WRAP-UP // Final thoughts and prayer

BIBLE CONVERSATION *(10 minutes)*

The goal of the Bible conversation is not to exhaust the topic, but merely to introduce it. We want people to explore the Bible passage and talk about one or two good questions that create a desire for more answers.

`SET-UP` As we've been doing every week, we want to start our time together by reading a passage from the Bible and thinking about it together. The passage we're going to read this week is 1 John 1:5–9.

`READ` *Have someone read 1 John 1:5–9 aloud.*

`ASK` Okay, let's make some basic observations about the passage. The basic contrast or metaphor is light and darkness.

What kinds of ideas are connected to "light" in this passage? List as many as you can find (*God, truth, fellowship, cleansing from sin*).

What kinds of ideas are connected to "darkness" in this passage? List as many as you can find (*lying, deception, sin, unrighteousness*).

So, practically, how would you describe what it means to "walk in the light"?

`TRANSITION TO ARTICLE` From these verses, it's clear that "walking in the light" is good and desirable. But walking in darkness is more deeply ingrained in us than we realize. This article is going to help us see some of the ways we walk in darkness instead of light.

ARTICLE *(10 minutes)*

`READ THE ARTICLE` *Read "An Honest Community" aloud together, taking turns at paragraph breaks.*

`TRANSITION TO DISCUSSION` Let's discuss this article for a few minutes.

DISCUSSION *(15–20 minutes)*

This article has some good concepts, and it's possible that the discussion will lead itself as people engage with those concepts. Notice that the questions below are focused on personal application. We don't want your group talking in vague generalities about why "people" put forward a false image; we want them talking personally about why they put forward a false image. Keep it personal, not general.

`ASK` Is there anything in the article that stood out to you or that you want to discuss further?

ASK What are some of the reasons—for you—that you want to appear a certain way to people?

ASK Why do you think "image management" feels safer and easier than being honest?

ASK How does this impact the depth of honesty we can experience as a group and our ability to love and serve others?

TRANSITION TO EXERCISE I want to end with "Speaking the Truth in Love," an exercise that will help us dig deeper into the dynamics of honesty in relationships.

EXERCISE *(20 minutes)*

The point of this exercise is to discover the idols underneath our reasons for being less than honest about ourselves and others AND to talk about how the gospel confronts those idols, enabling us to walk in the light with one another. Don't stop at discovering the idols. Show how the promises of the gospel apply so that people can forsake their idols and worship Jesus instead.

SET-UP *Read the paragraph at the top of the exercise.*

READ QUESTION 1 *Give everyone time to think of something specific.*

THEN, READ QUESTION 2 *and give a minute or two for your group to identify their particular idols. If you need to offer more of an explanation to the concept of idols, consider this description from Lesson 6 of* The Gospel-Centered Life:

> Underneath every external sin behavior is a heart idol—a false god that has eclipsed the true God in our thoughts or affections. . . . To identify your particular heart idols, ask: What do I love, trust, or fear? For example, if I fear being single, being in a relationship will probably be my idol (because it promises to deliver me from the "hell" of singleness). If I trust in having

enough, security will probably be my idol (because it promises that I'll never be without anything). If I love order and structure, control will probably be my idol (because if I'm in charge, I can make sure things are in order).

FINALLY, READ QUESTIONS 3 AND 4 *and process them together as a group. Here are some more thoughts from* The Gospel-Centered Life *(Lesson 6) about seeing the significance of the gospel as it relates to our idols.*

Reflecting on the "sin beneath our sin" shows why the gospel is essential for true heart change. It's possible to repent of surface sins for a lifetime yet never address the deeper heart issues behind them! At the moment I sin, I have already broken the first commandment. An idol has taken God's place in my soul. I need to apply the gospel by (1) repenting of my deep heart idolatry and (2) believing—that is, turning my mind toward the specific gospel promises that break the power of my characteristic idols.

Take the surface sin of gossip as an example. Let's say that I have identified respect as the dominant idol that drives me to gossip. After I acknowledge my sin and repent of it, I exercise faith in two ways. First, I pause and worship Jesus because he laid aside his right to be respected, becoming humbled to the point of death (Philippians 2:5–11). [In the Exercise, we call this **"Looking to Jesus."**]. Second, I remind myself of the gospel truth that I no longer need to crave the respect of others because I have the approval of God through faith in Jesus (2 Corinthians 5:17–21). Whether people respect me or not is immaterial: God's grace has freed me from demanding my own respect, and now I live for the fame and honor of Jesus (1 Corinthians 10:31). [In the Exercise, we call this **"Believe the Gospel."**]

For a brief treatment of the examples in the exercise, see the chart on the next page.

TRANSITION TO WRAP-UP I really appreciate everyone's willingness to talk about this. I think we all want more honesty in our relationships, and a good place to go from here would be to pray toward that end. Let's pray not just for ourselves as individuals but for our group as well. Let's ask for God's help to seek honesty and transparency as a group and to be willing to let God show us idols we might have as a community that get in the way of God's purposes for us.

WRAP-UP
Questions, Comments, Prayer

A GRACE-FILLED COMMUNITY

FORMAT OVERVIEW

I.   BIBLE CONVERSATION // Read and talk about the passage(s)

II. ARTICLE // Read "A Grace-Filled Community" together

III. DISCUSSION // Process concepts together

IV. EXERCISE // Apply the concepts using the "Growing in Grace" exercise

V.   WRAP-UP // Final thoughts and prayer

BIBLE CONVERSATION *(10 minutes)*

In the Bible discussion, your aim is for people to simply share their observations about the text and their initial reactions to the discussion questions. The article and exercise will go into more depth.

SET-UP We are going to read two short passages that have similar punch lines. We are going to talk about what it means to have a grace-filled community, so as we read them, look for aspects of grace in these stories.

READ *Ask two people to read Luke 5:27–32 and Luke 7:36–47 aloud.*

ASK What are some characteristics of grace that you see in each passage?

ASK Where do you see the characters in these narratives *not* expressing grace?

TRANSITION TO ARTICLE Let's explore this topic in greater depth in "A Grace-Filled Community."

ARTICLE *(10 minutes)*

READ THE ARTICLE TOGETHER *Read "A Grace-Filled Community" aloud, taking turns at paragraph breaks.*

TRANSITION TO DISCUSSION Let's talk about what it means to be a grace-filled community.

DISCUSSION *(15–20 minutes)*

ASK Have you ever been in a community where you felt accepted (not perfectly, of course, but genuinely)? What made you feel that way?

ASK How many of you tend toward some aspect of pride as it was laid out in this article? Which scenario or description reminded you of yourself?

ASK How many of you tend toward some aspect of fear as it was talked about in this article? Which scenario or description reminded you of yourself?

ASK On a scale from 1 to 10 (1 being low, 10 being high), how grace filled would you say our community is? Why did you choose the number you did?

TRANSITION TO EXERCISE I think it's helpful to be honest about this topic, but let's spend the rest of our time actually seeking change. "Growing in Grace" is an exercise designed to help us reflect more deeply on how the Holy Spirit can change us.

EXERCISE *(20 minutes)*

SET-UP *Read the paragraph at the top of the exercise.*

Give people a minute to look through the exercise. Then let the conversation flow from there. Your job as the group leader is to help people identify their selfish tendencies and the ways they hinder the goal of a truly grace-filled community. But don't stop there. Make sure you get to the good news of how a gospel-driven acceptance would be different. Some potential follow-up questions might be:

ASK Which of these sinful tendencies (left column) do you see most often in yourself?

ASK How does this keep you from truly accepting others? Are you grieved by this?

ASK What aspects of Spirit-driven acceptance (right column) do you find compelling? What excites you or motivates you about being part of a community like that?

ASK As a group, are we characterized by any of these sinful tendencies in ways that hinder us from being a truly grace-filled community? How should we respond to that?

ASK I think it's easy for us to *agree* that we should be a community like this without really *longing* for it or doing the hard work it takes to cultivate it. Why is that?

Close your group by praying for more of the Spirit's presence and power in your community.

WRAP-UP

Questions, Comments, Prayer

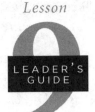
A MISSIONAL COMMUNITY

FORMAT OVERVIEW

I.   BIBLE CONVERSATION // Read and talk about the passage(s)

II. ARTICLE // Read "A Missional Community" together

III. DISCUSSION // Process concepts together

IV. EXERCISE // Apply the concepts using the "Living on Mission" exercise

V.   WRAP-UP // Final thoughts and prayer

BIBLE CONVERSATION *(10 minutes)*

SET-UP We are talking about what it means to live on mission with God and what keeps us from doing that. As we read this passage, look for how it speaks to those two issues.

READ *Have someone read 2 Corinthians 5:14–21 aloud.*

ASK What does this passage say about our identity and calling as missionaries? What stands out to you? *This question has a theological bent: What is true about us with regard to the mission of God?*

ASK What does it mean to be an "ambassador"? What does it mean that God makes his appeal through us? What are the implications for daily life? *These questions have a practical bent: What would it look like to live out our identity and calling as missionaries or "ambassadors"?*

`ASK` What are some ways you live like a missionary? How does that concept challenge you? *These questions have a personal bent: How does this reality/concept strike you personally?*

`TRANSITION TO ARTICLE` The article "A Missional Community" is going to help us reflect on what it means to live life for God and for his mission. Let's read it together and then talk more about the concepts it raises.

ARTICLE *(10 minutes)*

`READ THE ARTICLE TOGETHER` *Read "A Missional Community" aloud, taking turns at paragraph breaks.*

`TRANSITION TO DISCUSSION` Before we jump into the exercise, let's talk about a few concepts from the article.

DISCUSSION *(15–20 minutes)*

Because mission is about our heart before it is about our words and deeds, it is important to ask some reflective or diagnostic questions. You may not choose to use all of these, but we wanted to give you multiple angles to consider.

`ASK` Have you seen any of these **false perceptions about mission** in yourself (either now or in the past)? What effect did they have on your commitment to mission—or your fruitfulness in mission?

`ASK` "Mission means moving toward others . . . ." What do you find **exciting** about that and what do you find **challenging**?

`ASK` What do you think it means, practically speaking, to increasingly orient your life around the mission of God?

TRANSITION TO EXERCISE This week's exercise, "Living on Mission," is going to give us a lot to talk about, so I want to spend the rest of our time there.

EXERCISE *(20 minutes)*

This week's exercise will likely generate a frank, honest, and maybe even humbling conversation about the missional strengths and weaknesses of your group. So, before leading it: (1) confess to God any identity struggles you have that might cause you to be discouraged by or resistant to critique, and (2) work through the questions yourself and anticipate what people might say.

Before starting the exercise, decide which context you want the group to assess (their community group, their church, their mission team, etc.). A helpful hint: ONLY have them assess a context they actually have the power to change. For instance, if you are a community group leader within a church, don't have the group assess the church as a whole. Such assessments tend to lead to vague generalizations instead of actions leading to change. Instead, have them assess the community group for which they (as members) and you (as the leader) have direct responsibility.

Notice that after each set of questions, under "ACT," we ask: "Who is going to lead?" This is your chance to delegate responsibility and help people create solutions to the problems they identify. DON'T take the burden of change upon yourself. Rather, as people identify places they'd like the group to grow, invite them to take responsibility for change.

Read the paragraph at the top of the exercise handout and work through the questions together. As the leader, you can decide whether to work through all the questions or to focus on a few. Just make sure that you don't skip the REPENT-BELIEVE-ACT section.

WRAP-UP

Questions, Comments, Prayer

mission
propelled by good news

At Serge we believe that mission begins through the gospel of Jesus Christ bringing God's grace into the lives of believers. This good news also sustains and empowers us to cross nations and cultures to bring the gospel of grace to those whom God is calling to himself.

As a cross-denominational, reformed, sending agency with more than 200 missionaries and 25 teams in 5 continents, we are always looking for people who are ready to take the next step in sharing Christ, through:

- **Short-term Teams**: One- to two-week trips oriented around serving overseas ministries while equipping the local church for mission

- **Internships:** Eight-week to nine-month opportunities to learn about missions through serving with our overseas ministry teams

- **Apprenticeships:** Intensive 12–24 month training and ministry opportunities for those discerning their call to cross-cultural ministry

- **Career:** One- to five-year appointments designed to nurture you for a lifetime of ministry

Serge Grace at the Fray   **Visit us online at: serge.org/mission**

www.newgrowthpress.com

spiritual
renewal
resources for you

Disciples who are motivated and empowered by grace to reach out to a broken world are handmade, not mass-produced. Serge intentionally grows disciples through curriculum, discipleship experiences, and training programs.

Resources for Every Stage of Growth

Serge offers grace-based, gospel-centered studies for every stage of the Christian journey. Every level of our materials focuses on essential aspects of how the Spirit transforms and motivates us through the gospel of Jesus Christ.

- **101**: The Gospel-Centered Series
  Gospel-centered studies on Christian growth, community, work, parenting, and more.

- **201**: The Gospel Transformation Series
  These studies go a step deeper into gospel transformation, involve homework and more in-depth Bible study

- **301**: The Sonship Course and Serge Individual Mentoring

Mentored Sonship

For more than 25 years Serge has been discipling ministry leaders around the world through our Sonship course to help them experience the freedom and joy of having the gospel transform every part of their lives. A personal discipler will help you apply what you are learning to the daily struggles and situations you face, as well as, model what a gospel-centered faith looks and feels like.

Discipler Training Course

Serge's Discipler Training Course helps you gain biblical understanding and practical wisdom you need to disciple others so they experience substantive, lasting growth in their lives. Available for onsite training or via distance learning, our training programs are ideal for ministry leaders, small group leaders or those seeking to grow in their ability to disciple effectively.

Serge Grace at the Fray   **Find more resources at serge.org**

resources and mentoring
for every stage of
growth

Every day around the world, Serge teams help people develop and deepen a living, breathing, growing relationship with Jesus. We help people connect with God in ways that are genuinely grace-motivated and increase desire and ability to reach out to others. No matter where you are along the way, we have a series that is right for you.

101: The *Gospel-Centered* Series

Our *Gospel-Centered* series is simple, deep, and transformative. Each *Gospel-Centered* lesson features an easy to read article and provides challenging discussion questions and application questions. Best of all, no outside preparation on the part of the participants is needed! They are perfect for small groups, those who are seeking to develop "gospel DNA" in their organizations and leaders, and contexts where people are still wrestling with what it means to follow Jesus.

201: The *Gospel Transformation* Series

Our *Gospel Transformation* studies take the themes introduced in our 101-level materials and expand and deepen them. Designed for those seeking to grow through directly studying Scripture each *Gospel Transformation* lesson helps participants grow in the way they understand and experience God's grace. Ideal for small groups, individuals who are ready for more, and one-on-one mentoring, *Gospel Identity, Gospel Growth,* and *Gospel Love* provide substantive material, in easy-to-use, manageable sized studies.

The *Sonship* Course and Individual Mentoring from Serge

Developed for use with our own missionaries and used for over 25 years with thousands of Christian leaders in every corner of the world, Sonship sets the standard for whole-person, life transformation through the gospel. Designed to be used with a mentor, or in groups ready for a high investment with each other, each lesson focuses on the type of "inductive heart study" that brings about change from the inside out.

Serge Grace at the Fray

Visit us online at serge.org

www.newgrowthpress.com